The SIMPLIFY! Collection

Strategies and tips to get the right
things done every day

Bethanne Kronick

& Kim Greenwood

The SIMPLIFY! Collection, Strategies and Tips to Get the
Right Things Done Every Day

ISBN-10:069255596X
ISBN-13:978-0-6925-5596-5(SIMPLIFY!)

DEDICATION

To all our friends and clients. Hoping that there is always time in your day to do something that makes you smile, gives you joy and allows you to have an impact on the world.

Table of Contents

Foreword   v

Introduction   xi

SIMPLIFY! Terms and concepts
you'll see throughout the book: xiv

PRODUCTIVITY BEST PRACTICES   1

Take 5 – A Habit a Day to Get Started   3

Routines – Secret Weapons for Productivity   7

Start Strong – The Importance
of Morning Routines   13

Fab 4 Productivity Challenge   17

Find a Calendar System that Works   21

Strategies for a Productive
& Eco-Friendly Office   25

10 Ways to Invest 10 Minutes to Get Stuff Done!   31

Hit Your Mark – Setting Goals You Can Reach   35

Quick Tips to Save Time Every Day   41

**USING TECHNOLOGY TO
SUPERCHARGE PRODUCTIVITY**   45

Tap into the Power of Your Technology   47

Tips for Effective Emails   51

Mobile Manners   55

Time to Unplug - Tips for Technology Breaks   61

Feeling Sucked In by Social Media?   65

OFFICE SPACE AND ORGANIZATION   69

Filing 411 – Tips to Organize Your Files   71

Spring Cleaning Any Time of the Year   77

Power Purge   81

WORKING WITH OTHERS   85

Gold Medal Teams   87

Meetings that Matter   91

Is Your Message Clear?
Effective Communication   95

Building Productive Teams   99

PRODUCTIVITY PITFALLS   101

Are You Sabotaging Your Own Productivity?   103

Minimize Distractions   109

What is Procrastination Costing You?   111

Tools for Fighting Procrastination   117

How to Be Productive in Times of Chaos   121

Plugging those Pesky Time Leaks   125

Bust the Clutter!   129

TAKING CARE OF YOU! 133

Staying Productive During the Holidays 135

Simple Gift Giving Ideas 139

Ready for a break?
Staying Productive During Vacation Season 143

Scheduling for Success at Home 147

Making Time to Live Your Passions 151

Energize Naturally 157

Healthy Habits for Productivity 161

The Importance of White Space 167

Adding and Changing Habits 171

Need to Unplug? 175

Boost Your Brain Power 179

About the Authors 185

Gratitude 187

Endnotes 189

THE SIMPLIFY! COLLECTION

Foreword

When I was approached by Bethanne Kronick to write a foreword to their book, *The Simplify! Collection*, I was a little hesitant. After all, it was simply a compendium of time management and organizing tips extracted from past issues of their newsletter. But when I started reading, I realized the real value of simplicity – quick, readable and practical tips devoid of all the ponderous prose normally found in books on the same topic.

You don't have to plough through pages of background material, case studies or statistics to get to the meat of the ideas. Take them or leave them; they're laid out for you in simple, understandable terms – each one with a payoff for those who can apply it their particular situation.

For example, their suggestions on batching tasks is a

strategy that consumes less energy and prevents mental fatigue. It allows one to use the same areas of the brain and waste energy switching back and forth from one task to another, making frequent and unrelated decisions. I live by the concepts of batching and scheduling as described in their book.

And take their suggestions about the importance of natural lighting in your work area. Natural lighting from the sun is an environmental factor that can affect our health and personal performance. It improves cognitive performance alertness and mood. This is something I practice in my own workspace having moved my office from a windowless room to an area with ample natural light. Making sure natural lighting is available can improve performance and help to prevent health issues and daytime fatigue. It's a small change that can make a big impact.

I was delighted to see the authors provide tools for fighting procrastination. We are not alone in our tendency to procrastinate. After analyzing psychological literature, Piers Steel, a *University of Calgary* psychologist, concluded that 95 percent of people admit that they sometimes procrastinate. In

Bethanne and Kim's book you will find many tools to help with your procrastination problem – including over a dozen websites that offer helpful programs to address procrastination.

I'm sure you will find the guidelines for email and cell phone use of value. In his 2014 book *The Power of Forgetting*, Mike Byster says the average working professional spends roughly 23% of the workday on email, and glances at the inbox about 36 times an hour. And figures quoted in the book, *In Search of Balance* by Richard A. Swenson, indicate that typical corporate users send and receive about 167 messages daily and will spend 30% of their day creating, organizing, reading and responding to email. The tips and strategies can help many who are looking to break the cycle of repetitively checking email and getting bogged down in our inboxes.

We can all use a little help when it comes to cell phones. A study of over 200 students at the *University of Rhode Island* found they were losing an average of 45 minutes of sleep each week because of their cell phones. A *Wall Street Journal* article titled *BlackBerry Orphans* discussed how these gadgets were intruding on families and how children were feeling neglected. Psychologists reported that electronic devices were becoming a topic of conversation in family therapy sessions. When I was young, wives used to complain about husbands reading the paper at the kitchen table during meal time. Now it seems that Smartphones are the distraction of this generation and we are unfortunately, passing bad habits on to our kids as well.

And who can't use some guidelines for using social media? *Facebook*, the largest social networking site, was launched at *Harvard University* in 2004. Explosive growth in this form of media now means that as of 2014, there were 1.32 billion active users spending an average of 40 minutes a day on Facebook.

You may be one of those thousands of people who get bogged down with meetings. Hours of productivity are lost every week by poorly run meetings. This doesn't need to be the norm when strategies are implemented to improve focus and results from meetings. Bethanne and Kim provide help in their section on "Meetings that Matter."

They also help you avoid productivity pitfalls, such as multitasking. As mentioned in their book, the brain cannot do two tasks at the same time. It actually switches rapidly back and forth between one task and the other. Although the brain is only absent from either task for a fraction of a second, that brief absence could result in significant losses of productivity, poor overall results and unnecessary expenditures of effort.

Technology provides plenty of opportunities to multitask. A smartphone, for example, might allow you to leave work early and watch your son's soccer game; but you are still connected to your office and not fully present while your son is performing on the field.

We obviously need this reminder. 91% of Americans watch TV while they eat, 26% admit that they often eat while driving, and 35% eat lunch while they're at their desks while reading, working on a computer or making and receiving phone calls. The strategies shared for being present in the moment remind us that time is a valuable resource to be invested, not split between several tasks at once.

I am amazed by the number of areas covered in this brief book. I have only mentioned a few of them. There are guidelines for filing, organizing your office and even communicating. The authors include ways to plug time leaks, deal with clutter, boost your brain power – and get this – even how to be productive in times of chaos.

In keeping with their philosophy of keeping things simple, the authors have created a detailed table of contents page so the reader can quickly pick and flip to those areas of greatest interest to them. No need to start at the beginning with this book.

But I strongly suggest you eventually read it all. Whether you are concerned about your personal life or your professional life, your time or your health and well-being, there's something here for you. Don't miss it.

Harold Taylor
author of *Making Time Work for You*,
Partner in *TaylorInTime.com*

Introduction

Live simply. Simply live.

Four words that define our purpose at SIMPLIFY!
Life's valuable lessons about the significance of time
often come wrapped in challenge. A sudden loss,
illness or unexpected change in life circumstances
can force us to seriously contemplate how we are
investing the minutes and hours of our days. The best
case scenario is that we can reflect on this without
the prompt of a life crisis and make positive changes
in proactive vs. reactive ways.

One way or another, we'll have to jump off the
furiously spinning hamster-wheel of life and make
some changes or we'll simply run out of energy.
SIMPLIFY! was born out of the realization that many
of us are struggling with making the right choices
about the time we have to invest. Rather than waiting

for life to throw us a curve ball that forces a radical change in our habits, wouldn't it be great if we could make small changes to see big results in our ability to have more time for the things and people we love? The SIMPLIFY! team is passionate about helping busy people do just that. We provide coaching and training in strategies, systems, tools and habits that allow people to meet their goals and have the time to pursue their true passions.

Why does it matter? We are passionate at SIMPLIFY! about helping our clients get the most from their most valuable resource – time. Time is a precious and finite resource we can't multiply, purchase or get back so our choices on how we invest it have significant results in our professional and personal lives.

The SIMPLIFY! team looks at the best of the classic strategies and new trends in productivity, focus and at making the most of our time. Our monthly newsletter has featured the best of our proven strategies and tips for getting the *right* things done and keeping focused even on the craziest of days.

In the following pages we've collected a few of our most popular articles including best tips, strategies and disciplines on how to improve productivity. Not just to get more done, but to get the important stuff done. Not just to finish earlier, but to finish well and to ensure we have time for those people, projects, activities and passions that fuel us and make life worth living.

A life SIMPLIFIED! We hope these tips and strategies help you get closer to that goal every day.

Bethanne & Kim

SIMPLIFY! Terms and concepts you'll see throughout the book:

Focus Time – In today's overly busy and information-saturated world, it can be difficult to find enough time to get your work done. Set aside designated blocks of time called "Focus Time" to work on projects that require higher levels of focus and attention. Block segments of 30-90 minutes at a time and make an effort to limit interruptions, distractions and conscientiously avoid the temptation to multitask. The results from this practice allow for getting highest priority tasks done, with higher quality and faster progress with less stress. Use a desktop timer to help track your time. To maximize your commitment, we encourage blocking Focus Time as an appointment on your calendar so it doesn't get bumped by other lower value tasks. Take it even a step further and make it a recurring appointment on your weekly calendar.

Action System – There are many options (paper or digital) to track active projects and tasks. Choose a paper calendar, your email program's calendar, a task list (paper or electronic), an action folder located in your email folders, a tickler file or a combination of these options. Having a system will help ensure you keep on top of individual and recurring projects.

5 Decisions – A strategy to process incoming information including: email, incoming digital and paper documents, voicemail, requests of yourself or from others. Make one of five decisions to process each item: **toss or delete**, **delegate or forward**, **do it now or reply**, **file for reference or transfer to your Action System**.

Capture Cards – Stay on track in meetings and during focused work times by using some form of capture media for "dumping" thoughts and ideas from your brain that are not necessary for the immediate work but are things you want to be sure to remember. Use notecards, a small pad, a tape recorder or an electronic device to record thoughts, ideas and to-do's to revisit later and enter in your Action System.

Today's Top Three Must-Do's – During your daily planning time, determine three high priority tasks that are critical for you to accomplish. We recommend writing them down each day and keeping them visible to help keep you on task.

PRODUCTIVITY BEST PRACTICES

Time is what we want most, but what we spend worst.
– William Penn

Do you ever wish you had a fairy godmother that could wave her magic wand and slow down time? Wouldn't that be great?

You could put in a full day at the office, get everything done on your to-do list, exercise, read your favorite books, call your friends and family, get those chores done and have time to pursue new passions before the hours run out of your day.

Sadly, there is no magic wand or secret formula to freeze time so you can get it all done. Instead, we offer some basic strategies and disciplines that can help you find ways to be more effective with the precious time you have.

We hope these articles from our monthly newsletter on the topic of **Productivity Best Practices** inspire you to make changes in how you invest your most valuable resource — time. However, new habits and practices take time to develop so just reading these tips and learning about productivity strategies won't be enough. It will take some action on your part to make real changes but it's an investment that will bring great dividends if you are consistent and committed to making positive changes.

Are you ready? Let's go!

■   ■   ■

Take 5 – A Habit a Day to Get Started

All too frequently we have grand plans to make major overhauls to our work spaces and systems. It's more often smaller, sustainable changes that we are able to keep up with and bring results. Here are five easy strategies for improving your productivity — one for each day of the week.

Mondays — Take 10-15 minutes to plan your week ahead.

Determine your top three "must-do's" for the day. Review your schedule for upcoming meetings and put tasks that need to be completed in your Action System. Block **Focus Time** on your calendar for to-do's and projects. It's critical to plan ahead for projects or you will find your time slipping away dealing with interruptions and the priorities of others. Working without a plan is like going on a road trip without a map — who knows where you'll end up and how many times you'll get lost or turned around along the way.

Tuesdays — File and process paperwork to eliminate stacks and piles.

Create new folders for reference or project files if necessary. Also create digital folders to organize emails and documents for projects so you can find them easily. Schedule this time weekly so documents (paper and digital) don't stack up.

Wednesdays — Schedule time for reading and research you need for pending projects or improving your skills.

Look through journals, articles, online tutorials or webinars that can support your professional development. Catch up on reading the digital articles, newsletters and information you've been moving into your "To Read" folder, as well as the hard copy publications and documents you've been setting aside.

Thursdays — Block time to process the week's email out of your inbox and into appropriate folders if you've gotten behind during the week.

If you don't have time to draft responses to emails, let the sender know you have received their email and communicate when you'll be sending a response. (Make sure you place the item in your action file or on your task list for attention.) Take time to evaluate the emails you receive from organizations or companies on a regular basis (informational or sales related). Unsubscribe from those you no longer need or want.

Fridays — Organize your workspace before leaving for the week.

Focus on tidying up your space so when you come back on Monday, you will be energized to start the week ready to work. Finish pending projects if possible and bookmark where you left off on those that are unfinished so you can quickly resume working on them the following week.

You might need to adjust the order of these tips to better fit your work flow but implementing these tips will help you build some habits that will keep you on track. If you commit to taking on these simple steps for a month, you'll enjoy the benefits all year long!

Routines – Secret Weapons for Productivity

Do you find yourself wishing for super powers to make yourself productive? Even super heroes have tools they use to boost their super abilities (the Batmobile and Wonder Woman's invisible plane are favorites on our superhero wish lists!).

Routines can be one of your best tools to boost productivity on a day-to-day basis where lost minutes and hours can really add up. Here are a few tips for creating routines that will give your days a boost.

Evaluate: Review the Scene of the Crime

What current routines do you have? Which ones are working? Which ones do you seem to get "lost" in (you start them but they never seem to get done)? Try keeping a log on your desktop and honestly tracking your activities for three days to see where your time is going. Track how long recurring tasks take so you are sure to allot enough time for them. Look for repeated activities that might be stream-lined, automated or batched for productivity.

Delegate: Sidekicks are a Big Part of Superhero Success

Often we find ourselves doing things because we've always done it that way. Are there tasks you can delegate to others in your organization who might be able to complete them faster (and, let's be honest, maybe better)? If you can, let go of some of your less productive routine tasks and allow others take care of them. It will give you more time to pursue the important projects.

Automate: Utilize the Superhero Tools to Get More Done

Schedule reminders and events in your calendar program to keep you on track for recurring tasks. Create checklists for these projects so you are not losing time asking, "What's the next step?" If you're not comfortable with using electronic programs for this, consider creating a paper checklist and make copies to use each time the project comes around. Many of the programs we use daily for email, calendar and project management have great tools built in for productivity. Learn how to use your "gear" to get the most out of your day!

Be Flexible: Avoid the Kryptonite Effect of Routines

Just like Kryptonite can render Superman powerless, being too enslaved to routines can hinder personal and professional growth. Before you say, "I just COULD NOT start my day without checking email first thing in the morning..." why not give it a try? (Experts say checking email first is one of the foremost productivity traps. Try working on an important project for the first 30-40 minutes of your day and see how much more productive you will be!) Routines help us by keeping us on track but if they start getting in the way of growth (personal and professional) they are no longer working for you — they are working against you.

Make Movement in Your Day a Routine

Research is showing that the many hours spent sitting at our desks are contributing to some major health issues for workers. Exercise on a regular basis and make it a routine part of your day. Establish routines to get you out of your chair and moving during your work day. Set a timer or create calendar reminders that will appear on your screen to take a break. Try "walking meetings" when appropriate to add opportunities to walk and move during your day.

Just Do It!

Use the power of motivation to work on your routines. If you don't already have a "beginning of your workday" and an "end of your workday" routine, start there. What three things do you need to do to start your day well? What three things do you need to do at the end of your work day to set yourself up for success the next day? Write them down and try following them for at least a week. Evaluate how they worked, make tweaks and follow them for another week. Before long, you should begin to see the benefits of having these routine habits to get you started and to help you finish your work each day.

Take a note from our favorite superheroes and use your best tools to take back your time from the villains of disorganization, interruptions and procrastination!

Start Strong – The Importance of Morning Routines

With a little bit of planning, morning routines can be a valuable tool for improving productivity. Try these tips for starting new ones or refining those you already use to start your day.

Consider Reminders for Getting Out the Door in the Morning With All You Need

They can be as simple as Post-it® notes on the door frame or reminders on your phone. (This works great for **all** members of your household!)

Create a "Landing Space" for Items You Need

Keep items for work in one place (or in the same place each day) so they are easy to collect and you have everything for the day ahead. Designate a basket, bench or box and use it consistently to reduce time spent looking for items you need each morning.

Write Down your Top Three Must-do's for the Day

Start each day with this valuable habit and it will help you keep focus when distractions arise. (You'll also feel great when you can check each item off through the day!)

Tackle High-focus Tasks in the Morning

Take some of your best energy in the morning to devote to projects that require higher amounts of focus. Make a goal of finishing at least one of your top three must-do items before checking email.

Batch Tasks for Efficiency

Group your tasks together such as replying to voicemail, filing and email so that you can minimize the need to switch between tasks every few minutes.

Start Each Day with Inspiration!

Find a resource to encourage and support you in your efforts. Favorite quotes, devotionals or readings can help you start strong. Our book, *Simplify One Day at a Time - 365 Ways to Improve Productivity* contains daily entries with practical tips for productivity and inspiration can put you in "the zone" for making the most of each day![i]

Try a few of these in your own morning routines and reap the rewards of getting more done with less stress each day!

■   ■   ■

Fab 4 Productivity Challenge

We often hear from clients who are ready to make changes to help improve their productivity as they move into a new year. (Getting organized and becoming more productive is one of the top three resolutions each year!) You can take advantage of a fresh start at any time of the year but it's important to have a plan or your best intentions can easily fall by the wayside. Here is a *"Fab Four Challenge"* for any time of the year. Try implementing one of these challenges each week for a month and reap the rewards of success!

Week #1 — Change Up a Stale Routine

We are creatures of habit and often get caught in ruts: doing things a certain way because that's the way we've always done it. Find one routine that you think you can improve upon this month. Maybe it's getting up an hour earlier to get more done at home in the morning before you leave for work so you can truly relax when you get home. Or perhaps it will be taking breaks on a regular basis and getting up to stretch and move around. Be creative but practical and give yourself time to let the new routine become habit!

Week #2 — Create Folders for Your "Stacks"

Statistics say that we can lose up to almost an hour a day looking for information we need! This week create and label folders for your projects and documents. Create physical folders for the paper you manage and create email and digital folders for your digital documents. Where possible, be sure your physical folder and digital folder structures mirror each other. Make sure you are using a naming system that will be easy for you to use on a daily basis. The folders won't do much good if your system doesn't make sense.

Week #3 — Schedule a Reading Hour Each Week

Many of us have subscriptions to newsletters, magazines, journals and other publications that can help us in our professional development but they can also quickly become dust collectors in our offices or clutter in our inboxes if we're not careful. Schedule time each week to scan/read some of these resources and then toss/delete or give away/forward the ones you don't need any longer to help reduce clutter in your workspace.

Week #4 — Create Checklists for Repeated Tasks

Create checklists (paper or digital) for specific tasks that are frequently repeated. Use the checklists to ensure you are keeping on track with deadlines, to avoid reinventing the wheel.

Some possible checklists that might help save time or increase productivity might be:

- Planning time away from work (requests for coverage, setting auto responders on email and voicemail, contacting key vendors/clients, etc.)
- Planning meetings (agenda, invitations, facility and technology requests, catering, etc.)

- Online marketing (schedules for updates, back-ups, postings, monthly articles or content, etc.)
- Year-end tasks (reports, gathering documentation, archiving files, etc.)
- Looking for resources to create checklists? Check out www.listplanit.com, www.evernote.com , www.wunderlist.com, www.swipesapp.com, www.getfinish.com, and www.todoist.com.[ii]

It feels great to get a fresh start making improvements in our lives by being more productive. Who wouldn't love to recover some of the "lost" time for more fun and time with those we love. Take on this *Fab Four Productivity Challenge* to take back your time and get more out of life!

■   ■   ■

Find a Calendar System that Works

Time... don't you wish you had more of it? Calendars (whether they are in paper or electronic format) are excellent tools to make sure you get the most out of the minutes in your day. Making sure you have certain tasks scheduled can help build productive habits at work and in your personal life. Here are our best tips for scheduling for success.

Find a System That Works for You

Whether paper or electronic, find a calendar system that works best for you. One of the best strategies is to find one that works for both work and home related appointments (to avoid double booking yourself). Don't hesitate to change systems if you find that what you're using isn't working! Investing time in learning how to use electronic versions can have a large payoff as they can be synched on multiple devices. Calendar programs on your phone and tablet can help you from double-booking when you're away from your desk.

For those who prefer paper calendars (or those who have returned to using a paper calendar as many people have) there are many options on the market for different levels of tracking. Both types can work equally well if you find a system you can commit to using consistently.

Regularly Update Your Calendar

Choose one day a week to make sure your calendar is up to date with events, appointments and meetings. If you have a spouse, partner or children at home, consider a once a week "calendar check-in" where you update the family calendar with items to ensure you all know where you need to be. (If you use Outlook® or Google Calendar, consider sharing calendars to simplify this process.)

Schedule Specific Times to Respond to Emails, Then Leave It!

It can be easy in today's world to believe the

misconception that we need to **always** be available to respond to emails. Talk with your supervisor to see what is **really** required then aim for checking email at that frequency and put this on your schedule. People find that checking email 2-3 times per day or on an hourly basis is usually adequate, depending on their roles and responsibilities. Processing them in a batch will ultimately improve your overall focus and productivity by limiting the amount of time it takes to refocus after each interruption.

Schedule Blocks of Time for High Focus Projects

Let your phone go to voice mail and turn off email alerts so you can avoid interruptions. Close your door and notify coworkers when you'll be available and ask them to hold questions or phone calls. Consider working off-site or in a conference room to minimize disruptions even further.

Schedule Regular Times to Take Care of YOU!

Block time in your calendar for things like regular exercise, preventative health care (dentist, eye doctor, yearly check-ups) and vacation time. If you block these times out, it's more likely you will follow through on these important appointments that will ensure you have the energy and health to keep up with your busy schedule.

Your calendar can be a valuable ally in finding the time for the things you want to do! Try these strategies to make sure you are utilizing your time to get the most out of your days.

■   ■   ■

Strategies for a Productive & Eco-Friendly Office

The SIMPLIFY! team is passionate about the beauty and majesty of nature and we want to be sure we are doing our part to protect our valuable natural resources. We are so proud that the core message of our company, living life SIMPLIFIED!, matches up with the ideals of taking care of our planet and making sure our "stuff" doesn't rule us.

If you are looking for some ways to "green" up your daily routines and reduce your footprint on the world, here are a few of our favorite tips and strategies.

Reduce Your Paper

Consider these strategies to cut down on unnecessary printing:

- Transfer action items from key emails to your calendar or task list. If you choose to print the email itself, be sure to recycle the paper or use back sides of single sided printing for scratch paper.

- Save important documents as .pdfs and file the digital versions instead of printing them and putting them in paper files.

- Opt for email receipts from stores and vendors when possible.

- If you choose to print, set your printers to print double sided.

- Unsubscribe from mailers and catalogs that you can find online.

Green Your Commute

Consider taking public transportation and use the time on the bus or train to read, catch up on emails or just relax! If public transportation isn't an option, look into carpooling with coworkers or people in your community. (Sites like www.eRideshare.com and www.carpoolworld.comⁱⁱⁱ can hook you up with other folks looking to share rides. ***Please use caution and do your research before signing on with a*** *ride-share program or agreeing to a carpool option. Safety first!*) If you live near your office, consider riding your bike to work a few days a week and take advantage of fitting in a workout ***and*** reducing your carbon footprint at the same time!

Let There Be Light

According to a number of studies, the impact of lighting on productivity is substantial. Employees express higher levels of satisfaction and well-being when there are natural light options in the work place. If you have the ability to use the natural light of windows to help light your office, consider this a double dip for productivity and eco-friendly practices. If you don't have the option of windows, review your current lighting to make sure it is energy efficient and providing the best form of light for the environment.

Power Down

Shutting off your desktop computer can save as much as $90 worth of electricity in one year.[iv] That means a company of 100 could save up to $9000 per year in addition to adopting this green practice! The

Department of Energy recommends shutting off your monitor if you aren't going to use it for more than 20 minutes, and powering down your whole system at the end of the day. (You can adjust the settings on the computer to do this for you.) This green practice can save money and extend the life of your hardware.

Proactive Purchasing

There are lots of items needed to keep an office running. Evaluate what you *really* need and check into green options before making office supply purchases. Can you purchase recycled paper for your copier? Can areas of your organization share pieces of large equipment rather than each department having its own? Can you reuse file folders by purchasing new file labels or give binders and other supplies a new life? Making conscious decisions in our office purchasing can help keep clutter out of our offices, save money and help the environment; win, win, win! Looking for a place to start? Visit Office Depot's online Green Buying Guide[v].

Making a commitment to less waste and practicing earth-friendly office practices doesn't have to slow you down at work and can even help you in your efforts to a more productive day!

▦   ▦   ▦

10 Ways to Invest 10 Minutes to Get Stuff Done!

Feeling swamped and like there's not enough time to get everything done? We all have the same amount of minutes in a week and the challenge is not how we spend it, but how we *invest* it. The momentum of starting with a few short tasks can help you gain ground and see great strides in your productivity when it comes to the bigger projects. Here are 10 ways to invest 10 minutes to make progress on your lists and projects.

1. **Purge email folders.** Delete those that are no longer necessary. Weed out documents you no longer need from folders and archive documents that need to be stored longer.

2. **Purge a file folder or two**. Get rid of paper documents you no longer need or purge electronic documents that are out of date.

3. **Clean off your computer desktop.** Remove the visual clutter of miscellaneous files and icons on your desktop, leaving only those that you need easy access to frequently. Move documents to an appropriate folder and consider deleting documents and icons you no longer need.

4. **Clean out a drawer.** Whether at work or at home, making sure you can find what you need when you need it can save valuable time and help keep focus when working on projects.

5. **Evaluate your workspace.** Are there things on your desk you don't need that cause distraction? Make changes to improve your workflow and help keep you focused.

6. **Update your calendar.** Schedule your own **Focus Time** for larger, more complex projects, returning phone calls, professional development and reading/studying. Review

meeting times and locations. Add time for travel and prep if needed.

7. **Take a walk.** The dangers of sitting for long periods of time are well documented. Taking a walk can energize you, clear your head and prepare you for tackling a larger project on your must-do list.

8. **Create a list or template.** Create a checklist for repetitive tasks, a template for emails you often send or a list of resources you frequently use so that the information is in one, easy-to-access location.

9. **Review your contact lists.** Delete any entries that are out of date. Make a note of any contacts needing follow-up.

10. **Write a thank you note.** Building and maintaining relationships takes time but the investment always pays off.

10 minutes can seem like a small amount of time but it's enough to make significant progress when invested wisely.

Hit Your Mark — Setting Goals You Can Reach

It's important in our personal and professional life to embrace the act of DREAMING BIG and setting goals. Each year, schedule time to look toward the future and create a meaningful time of reflection on where you want to go personally and professionally. Having clear goals will help you focus and prioritize the activities that will help you reach your goals. Here are some tips to setting BIG GOALS and how to work toward reaching them.

Make it a Special Day

Because goal setting is such an important step in productivity and focus, we are big fans of scheduling specific time on the calendar to make it happen. A goal setting retreat can be a meaningful investment for you (or your team) as you look at personal and organizational goals. If possible, block off a half-day or full day to reflect on what is important to you and priorities in your life and work. It's a good day to get out of the office to do this in a fresh environment.

Create a List of Your Dreams

Think about the things you want to do, the person you want to be and the things you would like to add to your life (hopefully not "stuff" but experiences and those things that really matter). Consider both the professional/work side of your life and your personal life. Choose goals that will incorporate your passions and interests. Matching your goals to your passions will help you keep momentum as you do the hard work of meeting your goals. Dream BIG! ***Make sure you are aiming for what you really want.***

Create a Short List of Personal and Professional Goals

Look at your dreams and choose those you feel you have passion for and the ability to work toward as goals. Think about your career, financial goals, educational goals, physical and health goals, goals for your family, and goals related to following your passions.

Align Your Activities and Habits to Your Goals

Goals act as a road map to keep you from "dead-end" activities. Participating in an activity without a goal in mind is like driving aimlessly without a map or any idea of a destination. Matching your activities and habits with your goals leads to accomplishments and moving closer to your dreams.

Create a Plan to Reach Your Goals with Specific Steps

If your goal is to run a marathon but you've never even run a 5K, it will make sense to set some short-term goals as benchmarks on the way to running the marathon. Write down a plan breaking down your goals into smaller, achievable goals. Set short-term, mid-term and long-term goals that are linked to moving you closer to your big goals and dreams.

Make Reaching for Your Goals a Lifestyle

Work to adopt a mindset that allows you to consider how each activity is moving you closer to (or keeping you from) achieving your goals. Look at your habits, systems and processes for ways you can make progress in reaching your goals on a daily basis. What do you need to add that will help you reach your goals? What activities or habits need to be limited or removed to move you closer to your goals?

Accountability is Key

Working toward achieving our goals can be challenging. When the work gets hard, it can be a great encouragement to have someone cheering you on. Share your goals with a friend or colleague so they can help you during the hard times and celebrate with you when you succeed.

The Best Goals are S.M.A.R.T.

There is great wisdom in this old acronym. It's important your goals be articulated in ways that are specific, measurable, achievable, realistic, and timed. Write them down (including due dates) for accountability and to keep focused.

Take Time to Reflect and Celebrate

Schedule time quarterly or semi-annually to review

your goals, track your progress and make any necessary adjustments to your plan. These check-ins can be a valuable strategy to help you hit your mark! It's also important to take time to celebrate your accomplishments. Reflect on the strategies and habits that helped you meet those goals as you consider setting new goals. How can you capitalize on your success and use those habits to meet new goals?

Make this your best year yet! Take some time to invest in your future and set goals that will move you closer to your dreams.

▪   ▪   ▪

Quick Tips to Save Time Every Day

It's always a good practice to review how we are spending our time each day. Checking in can help us find the notorious time wasting activities in our days and help us refine our habits and systems to take back our time. Our goal is to invest those minutes and hours into worthwhile activities and things we **want** to do. Here are some helpful time hacks for getting more done, in less time with less stress.

Create an "Out the Door" List

This is a favorite tip borrowed from busy parents. Write a list on a Post-it® of things you'll need for the following day and put it on your door so you'll see it before you leave in the morning. Better yet, gather as many as you can in a central place as you think of them.

Use Recording Apps to Dictate Notes and Emails

Install a recording app on your phone to dictate emails, reminders, and things you don't want to forget. Some programs will even convert the recordings to text for you. Use this while waiting for appointments, in line to get gas, etc.

Cut Down on Unnecessary Screen Time

Set limits on your screen time so you can focus on what truly needs to get done. (This includes TV, Netflix, Facebook, Pinterest, Instagram, YouTube, other social media sites, online games and other non-work related online time.) A little digital recreation is fine but most of us wind up spending far more time than we planned on these activities and then we find ourselves in time crunches because we're rushing to catch up on our obligations.

Utilize the Top Three Must-Do's and Keep Them Handy All Day

We may sound a bit like a broken record, but we feel strongly about this core productivity tip. To make sure you're spending time on what's important and not just urgent (and maybe easier?), keep your three

must-do's list close and visible so you can stay
focused.

Drink Water, and Then Drink Some More

A fuzzy or tired brain is often a sign of dehydration.
Want to get more done? Keep yourself hydrated
throughout the day!

Find the short-cuts and hacks that work for you and
then utilize them to make sure every minute counts!
Here's to living each day with no regrets about how
we invest our most valuable resource—our time!

USING TECHNOLOGY TO
SUPERCHARGE PRODUCTIVITY

The first rule of any technology used in a business
is that automation applied to an efficient operation
will magnify the efficiency. The second is that
automation applied to an inefficient operation
will magnify the inefficiency.
– Bill Gates

Team SIMPLIFY! understands that our gadgets can be our best friends or our worst enemies when it comes to using our time well. These handy tools can help us track appointments, automate repeated activities, keep us connected and help answer important questions quicker than you can spell "G-o-o-g-l-e."

Technology has done much to allow greater pro-ductivity and connection but in return it has put unique demands for access on us that can make it feel like we are always "on the clock." The following articles are some of our best strategies for maximizing and managing the technology available to us making sure it helps us get the *right* things done in less time with less stress.

▨   ▨   ▨

Tap into the Power of Your Technology

Technology can be one of the best tools in our productivity arsenal. Here are some tips for maximizing the benefits of our tech tools.

Learn the Ropes

New technology can seem overwhelming at first. We can be tempted to learn just enough to get started and we may miss out on some of the helpful features that may take just a bit more time to learn. If you are going to invest in new hardware or software, remember you will want to invest in learning and mastering the technology. (Look for free classes through the retailer where you purchased the device, at your local library, or search for helpful videos online that can guide you through some of the features and tools available to you.)

Automate Repeated Activities

Look for ways your technology can help with tracking, connecting, creating and collaborating by automating recurring tasks. Think about ways to simplify email, your calendar, to-do lists and other areas of your work and life.

Go Paperless

Use the benefits of mobile technology to reduce your dependence on paper. Keep documents you need for reference or ongoing projects on an exchange server or cloud storage site that you will be able to access from anywhere.

Maximize the Cloud

New to the cloud? It's a magical place that allows you to store documents that you can access from almost anywhere you have a Wi-Fi connection with your technology (laptop, tablet and phone). You can allow others to access your files as well. Popular options are DropBox, GoogleDrive, Microsoft OneDrive, Apple iCloud Drive and Box. Talk to your IT support or research some of these sites to find the best fit for your needs (remember to find one you can use across your devices – phone, tablet and laptop or desktop).

Research Before You Purchase

There are many options for technology solutions and the choices seem to increase by the day! Before you go and buy the latest and greatest, take time to research products, software and services to be certain they will meet your needs. When adding technology, check to see if it will sync well with other devices, software and programs you use regularly.

Time invested in your technology can bring great payoff in productivity. Make sure the effort you are putting in to these gadgets brings you closer to your goals of maximizing your work time so you can spend time pursuing the things you are passionate about.

■   ■   ■

Tips for Effective Emails

The average professional spends up to 28 percent of their work week on emails[vi]. With that kind of time investment, it's important to craft emails that produce results. Try some of these tips to improve the readability of your emails and you may just recover a few of those hours for higher value projects.

Less is More

Think carefully about what you send, forward and copy. Ask, _is this email really necessary? Does this person really need it? Is the message or request for action clear?_

Make Sure Your "Ask" is Clear

If there is an action or follow-up required, clearly articulate the details and the due date. Get to the point quickly. Consider using bold font or separating the "ask" from other text to make sure it is clear.

Provide Clear Subject Lines

They should clearly indicate the topic and action requested in the email. Example: "**<u>Action</u>** - Please Submit Marketing Plan Updates by 5/15" or, "**<u>Request</u>** - Please Send November Sales Figures by 12/5".

Respond Promptly

You can encourage prompt responses by modeling the habit. If you have set times you check email (this is highly recommended for improved focus and productivity) you may even include this information in your signature text. *Example, "Your email is important to me. I check my email twice a day and try to respond to each one in 24 hours. If you need a more immediate response, please contact me by phone at..."*

Investing time in crafting effective emails can help improve productivity in many ways. Keeping your messages brief, calling out specific requests and responding promptly can help to maximize your efforts in this important tool for communication. If email is a struggle for you, consider options for training and coaching in this area to refine your strategies and practices for best results.

■　　■　　■

Mobile Manners

Cell phones can be useful tools for keeping connected but just like any piece of technology, there can be a dark side to these little mini computers we carry around in our pockets. To make sure the technology is helping and not hindering your productivity efforts (and your relationships), consider these strategies.

Safety First

ONLY use your phone while driving with the proper safety equipment (hands-free). Spend time learning your voice activated dialing so you can make calls safely from your car. Don't hesitate to pull over if you have technical challenges or if a conversation needs more attention and takes your focus off your driving.

Put Your Phone Away When Working

It was reported recently the average person checks their smart phone an average of 150 times per day![vii] Each time you check your phone it can take several minutes to get back on task. That can quickly eat away at your work time. Put your phone in a drawer, purse or backpack nearby so it is out of sight and check it only on specific breaks and lunch.

Develop a Strategy for Phones in Meetings

You might be checking work emails but others might perceive you are "checking out" and may make incorrect assumptions about your work ethic. It really is NOT effective multitasking to be answering emails during meetings (neither the meeting nor your emails are getting your full attention). If you feel the content of the meeting is not relevant to you, make a note to decline the invitations in the future or opt to send a delegate. A local company we work with recently implemented a "phones off" policy. They have experienced significant improvement in the productivity of their meetings, and the quality of discussion has improved as people are fully engaged and making eye contact!

Learn How to Silence Your Phone

As a courtesy to others, it is important to learn how to silence devices when at meetings, theaters, places of worship, performances, professional service providers and some eating establishments. If you must take a call while at one of these events or locations, be sure to step out to take the call so as not to disturb others.

Remember Common Courtesy

Limit use of your cell phone to appropriate spaces and times and avoid using phones for extended conversations in public places. Don't keep people waiting for you at the checkout, in restaurants, the carpool lane, etc.

Activate Your Filter

When taking or making calls in public places, your conversation is available for anyone within a few feet. Keep calls professional and avoid conversations that would reflect poorly on you or others in public places (really, anywhere - but especially in public!). Consider privacy/confidentiality issues when taking work calls in public places.

Set Boundaries

The trend seems to be for phones to be ever-present and always at hand. This can be a problem when our phones become a distraction when we need to be focused. Put phones away when your attention should be on people or other tasks at hand. Demonstrate courteous cell phone behavior to your colleagues and family. If necessary, make a polite request to put phones away when you are together.

Make Meals Tech Free

It can be easy to think technology needs to be on the table when eating meals alone and even when dining with others. Some swear by the "phones in the middle of the table" challenge - when you are at a restaurant, all phones go in the middle of the table. The first person to check for texts, emails or calls before the meal is over has to cover the bill! Commit to keeping phones in your pocket or bag during meals and enjoy the conversation. We all need digital breaks!

Take Time to Unplug

Make a practice of turning off, putting away or at the very least, limiting the use of your cell phone for work projects at home. More time online without breaks can have a negative impact on our productivity. Let colleagues know when you'll be offline. It can be as simple as a message in your signature line that explains that emails received after 5 p.m. will not receive a response until the following day.

It's important to follow the best practices of using these mighty gadgets. Without some specific boundaries, there is strong potential they can become addicting, time-sucking distractions instead of a productivity tool.

■   ■   ■

Time to Unplug -
Tips for Technology Breaks

Technology provides great help to us in our work and personal lives but sometimes it can feel like we are *always* plugged in. How do we know if it's time for a break? Is your phone or tablet the first thing you check in the morning and the last thing you check at night? If so, it might be time for a break. Here are a few tips to get you started.

Set Your Time Frame

If you're really dependent on your device and feel this will be a challenge, start with just an hour or two of being unplugged and then work yourself up to a full day. Commit to a set amount of time and ask for accountability from a family member or friend.

Plan Ahead

Pull data from devices you might need like schedules, phone numbers, directions, etc. If you will be offline for more than a day, consider leaving that information on your voicemail and/or in an auto response on your email letting people know you'll be offline.

Turn it Off and Put it Away

Part of the draw of many of our devices is that "instant" access. Turn your devices off and put them away so the temptation for a quick "peek" at email, news and social media isn't there. Put laptops and tablets in bags and phones in drawers.

Enjoy

Plan something for your digital break that you love to do. You are less likely to feel like you are in withdrawal from not having access to your devices if you are having fun.

Technology can be a great help in our efforts to be more productive and maximize our time but it can also turn into an energy drain on us if we are not careful. Taking time away is a great practice to ensure we are reaping the benefits of our technology without falling into unproductive and unhealthy habits. Take the challenge to power down, cut the cord and unplug on a regular basis!

■   ■   ■

Feeling Sucked In by Social Media?

According to recent surveys and reports, Americans are spending more of their online time on social networking sites than ever before. Some estimates say that up to 16 minutes of every hour we spend online is on a social network site (think Facebook, Twitter, LinkedIn, Instagram, Pinterest, Tumbler and YouTube as just a few examples).

While these sites can offer some strategic benefits for connecting and collaborating, they can also cause their share of problems. It is estimated that 6 out of 10 workers spend time on social network sites at work and the estimate value of time lost in the US from this expensive habit is 650 billion dollars per year (yes - billion with a "b").[viii] If you find yourself spending too much time on these types of sites, here are some strategies to help you make better choices with your online time.

Track Your Online Diet

Take the challenge to track your online activity for three days. How much time is really spent on work and emails and how much is checking your social media sites? You may be surprised to find out the amount of time you are spending on these sites.

Take Better Breaks

We often justify our social media visits as "breaks" in our work. Visiting social media sites doesn't really give our brain, eyes or our backs a break. (Getting up and moving away from our screens is a much more productive break.) Checking social media sites is more like just a different "task" and as a result, it takes us longer to get back to the original work we were trying to do.

Set Limits

If you are going online for personal or professional research, set the timer for 20 minutes. When the buzzer sounds, get up and step away from the screen for at least a 5 minute break. Think about how you want to use your time. Do you really want to be online for another 20 minutes or would your time be better spent doing something else?

Disable Your Internet

Programs such as Freedom [ix] (www.macfreedom.com) can help you set limits by temporarily disconnecting you from the internet for set periods of time. This is a favorite tool when you need some focused time on your laptop or device without the temptation of being able to go online.

If You Are Not Paying For a Product, You Are The Product

Remember this old adage as you post information on social media sites. They can be great tools for connecting and collaboration but ultimately the creators of these programs are interested in collecting data about consumers (you) and using the information to sell you things. *How much of your time and personal information are you willing to give away for free to these companies?*

Accountability can help us change negative habits into positive ones. If this is an area of struggle ask a mentor or friend to help you take steps to limit your time online. Your time is valuable! Spend it in ways that bring you closer to your dreams, goals and passions instead of on passive activities online.

* * *

OFFICE SPACE AND ORGANIZATION

Yesterday is gone. Tomorrow has not yet come.
We have only today. Let us begin.
– Mother Teresa

The 1990s movie, **Groundhog Day** told the story of a man who was stuck living the same day over and over again eventually learning how to make all the negatives and disastrous experiences turn to positives. (It took him a while though!)

It can sometimes feel like the quest to "get organized" is our own personal Groundhog Day. We work to get our piles in order, to get our office environment streamlined and then a crisis or busy season will throw us off and we feel like we are starting all over again.

Organization is more than just about positive aesthetics in your work space. The lack of organization can impact our performance, opportunities for advancement and our organization's bottom line. When we are spending time looking for things we need, that is time lost to higher value projects.

In the following section, you'll find strategies to improve office organization. Whether you are working in a cube, a corner office or from a desk in your kitchen, the principles are the same. Our space and the way we use it can play a significant role in our ability to focus, accomplish high-value work and make the most of our time. Here's to getting out of the Groundhog Day loop when it comes to our organization skills!

■　　　■　　　■

Filing 411 – Tips to Organize Your Files

It always feels good when we're done with the task of filing but sometimes it's hard to get the motivation to get the job started. We know we need to clean off our desks, get rid of the leaning stacks of files and papers, clean out the hundreds of emails in our inboxes and clean off our desktop. More than just feeling we "should" do this, there is evidence our environment can impact our ability to focus and maintain productivity. Filing is a great way to start the process. Here are some strategies for organizing files.

Make Filing Easy On the Eyes

Filing paper with row after row of manila folders in a drawer can be a bit like a diet of dry toast. It doesn't need to be that way! Consider using color to designate different types of files. Many office supply stores now carry folders in bright colors and patterns. Select a handful of colors to designate various large categories. Using color is an effective way to find the files you need but be cautious about going overboard so it doesn't become confusing. There may be a bit more of an investment than in the traditional manila folders but if the color helps you locate things quicker, the investment will pay off in the time you save. Another option is to use strategic placement of file tabs. Tabs on the left, center or right can indicate different categories or topics.

Build a Clear Labeling Structure

For paper files, create labels that are clear and easy to read so you can find them quickly. For electronic folders you access frequently, consider placing a hyphen or some type of punctuation at the beginning of the file name so they will appear at the top of the file list. Folders (paper or electronic) should have clear meaning to you so you can quickly place things where they can be found again.

As you develop your file structure, start by creating folders with the "big ideas" of your work and projects and then narrow from there to create sub-folders.

Create a digital filing system that will help you avoid storing reference items and documents in your inbox or on your desktop. Try to align your filing structure for paper and digital documents. The more they can mirror each other the simpler your filing will be.

Schedule Time on Your Calendar for Filing

Blocking just 15 minutes a week can help prevent the task from becoming an overwhelming process. Pick a time of day when you might already struggle with high focus projects (like right after lunch or right before heading home on Friday afternoons) and schedule time to file and process paper and electronic documents. If you need to schedule a longer period of time to catch up on large amounts of filing, consider listening to music for inspiration while you file to help the time go by faster.

Protect, Backup and Archive Your Data

Some organizations truly do need to keep excessive amounts of documentation but most of us keep more than we really need. If you work for an organization that requires you to keep large volumes of digital or paper information on file, work with your supervisors to clearly understand the archiving expectations and procedures.

If you have important paper documents, and you are a solo business owner, consider storing a copy in a second location as a back-up. If you work for a larger organization, make sure to research the requirements for retaining paper and digital files and archive when possible to keep your work environment efficient.

Ensure paper documentation is stored in appropriate containers, banker boxes, file boxes, cabinets, etc. Check to see if there are off-site storage options so you keep enough true "work space" in your office or cubicle. Always make sure you have a system in place to regularly back up and secure your data.

Filing regularly can keep you on track with projects, reduce clutter and help you find things faster. By implementing some of the above strategies you can keep on top of your piles and free up more time for higher value projects and pursuing your passions. A much better way to spend your time rather than looking for the piece of paper that you swear you just saw yesterday...

■   ■   ■

Spring Cleaning Any Time of the Year

At certain times of the year, you may find yourself with a bit more energy and motivation to tidy up your spaces. The calendar doesn't necessarily have to say March to feel like it's a good time to invest time **sprucing up your work space**. Here are some of our top tips for creating an organized work space that will save you time and ease stress.

Clear the Clutter!

Focus on eliminating unnecessary physical "stuff" in your work space. Get rid of the pens that don't work. Put things you don't use regularly in drawers instead of on your desktop. What about those items that tend to creep in our workspace like the four coffee mugs and those granola bars that have been sitting in your bottom drawer for two years? Take some time to clear the clutter and simplify your space.

Use a Physical Inbox and Outbox to Minimize the Clutter on Your Desk

Place the inbox in a spot where people can drop things for you without being disruptive. Place your outbox in a convenient location on or near your desk so that it's out of the way but you don't have to move far to reach it when you're ready to clear something off your desk for distribution. If you work in a predominantly digital environment, revisit your systems for your digital documents to ensure they are organized efficiently.

Minimize Visual Distractions

You know the list of company employees that has been on your wall for so long that many of them are no longer there? Get rid of it! Place other useful lists in a "quick reference" file or folder that is easily accessible. Take a look around your work space. Personal items (photos, certificates, quotes, etc.) are great to encourage us and create a positive atmosphere, but consider taking away things that cause distraction.

Purge Your Computer Desktop

Delete the icons for programs or documents you don't regularly use. They are just shortcuts that can be accessed through My Documents or Start>All Programs. Move documents into appropriate file folders.

Schedule 10 Minutes a Day to Keep Up on Organization

Go through a drawer, a handful of files, your email inbox, etc. Break organizing projects into ten minute chunks to get through them gradually. It's amazing how much progress you can make in just ten minutes and the amount of satisfaction you'll get from that small investment of time! Try scheduling this into your day at a regular time (like the 10 minutes before or after lunch). After a few weeks it will become a great habit!

Clearing the clutter (real and virtual) can go a long way in encouraging productivity. Consider a quarterly prompt on your calendar to spend time on your office space. Any time of year is a good time for spring cleaning!

※　　　※　　　※

Power Purge

Do you ever feel you are drowning in files? While there is value in ensuring you have resources you need for projects and tasks, **statistics tell us that 80% of the information we save or file is never looked at again!** That's a lot of space (physical and digital) to save unnecessary information. Schedule time to purge your paper and digital files using a few of our favorite strategies.

The Team That Purges Together...

We have seen great success in organizations that dedicate regular days during the year for organization and purging. If you can get your coworkers involved, schedule a casual day at work, order some pizza and make it a company- or department-wide project to get files trimmed down and organized. (If everyone is participating, you'll all be too busy to be sending email and creating more work during the day!)

Give Your Documents and Files an Expiration Date

There are times where we need to keep information for a while, but if your office is starting to look like an episode of the TV show **Hoarders,** consider starting the habit of writing a "toss by" date at the top of your files and documents. If you haven't referred back to the information within that time frame, chances are you won't need it again. (Or, if possible, store digital copies instead of hard copies to save space.)

Give Your Digital Filing Structure Some Attention

Don't forget to clean up the filing you do on your computer. Delete items you no longer need. Run regular scans and defragmentation software so you can keep your machine operating at its best. Create a system for backing-up files and update your anti-virus software regularly. Consult with your IT department on protocols and if you are a solo-preneur, find a reliable IT professional to assist you with this if you need help.

Be Ruthless

Remember that statistic we mentioned earlier? 80% of the items you save for reference will never be looked at again. It would be nice if we always knew which 20% we would actually need to keep but sometimes we have to use our best judgment and aggressively toss things so we don't wind up swimming in unnecessary paper. With today's easy access to information online, try to avoid keeping paper documents tracking information that can be found online. If you have a digital copy of a file, avoid saving paper versions to save space. The less you save the less you'll eventually have to purge!

Investing time in filing systems and purging practices can SIMPLIFY! your days and leave more time for higher value projects. Schedule your own power purge and celebrate the freedom that comes from letting go of things you won't need!

■   ■   ■

WORKING WITH OTHERS

Talent wins games, but teamwork and intelligence
wins championships.
- Michael Jordan

Many of us spend more hours with our colleagues than we do with our own families each week. Even if we work as a freelancer or solopreneur, our work likely has us connecting with others on a regular basis.

Workplace storylines have been at the core of several popular television shows. The popular sitcom, **The Office** created several seasons of hilarity looking at the quirky things that can happen when a diverse group of characters work in a small paper sales office. The dysfunctions of **The Office** were comedy genius, but in real life, dysfunctional teams can be a major stumbling block in our efforts to get the right things done at work.

It's important we learn and implement practices and systems that will help with productivity on an individual basis but when a group is working together with the same priorities and strategies to improve productivity, incredible growth and positive change can happen! There is great value in knowing how members of a team can support one another in efforts to focus on high value projects rather than diluting their efforts with lots of busy work and managing interruptions. When everyone is on the same page with how to make the most of their time, there is less stress, resources are maximized and goals are met.

Those offices where teams are sharing the same processes and practices may not have the crazy hijinks of the cast of *The Office*, but they are sharing smiles and high-fives as they GET STUFF DONE!

■   ■   ■

Gold Medal Teams

Like clockwork, every four years many of us will be yelling at our television sets.

It won't be because we disagree with the judges on our favorite reality show, or because we are lamenting the cancellation of our favorite comedies. It will be yells of, "Go. Go. GO! GO! GO!" and chants of "U-S-A! U-S-A!" that will be heard in living rooms across the country.

When the Olympics come around, we watch top-level athletes performing amazing feats of strength and discipline at their highest levels. As we seek to be top performers in our own fields, here are a few valuable lessons we can learn from them about building gold-medal teams.

Team Members Work in Their Strengths

As a leader, make sure you delegate tasks with forethought and planning based upon your team's strengths. Don't ask your weightlifter to walk the balance beam, and don't select your soccer player to take the platform dive. A team member working in their strengths will perform at higher levels and remain engaged in the project.

They Have Clear, Measurable Goals

Each athlete with a long-term goal of competing at the Olympics must accomplish many short-term goals in order to get there. Those short-term goals included other competitions and personal benchmarks they met along the way. In the same way, your team should have short-term and long-term goals clearly articulated so there is clear direction on where you are all heading. *(What is your Olympics?)*

There are Clear Expectations for Accountability and Communication

Athletes are accountable to coaches, sponsors, fans, and to their own families. Is your team on board with communication expectations and points of accountability? Does your team have systems in place to receive feedback from clients? How is that evaluated? Keeping all the key players on your team focused and working toward the same objective will save time, money and frustration and keep you on the road to reaching your goals.

There is a System for Tracking Progress

Hi-tech labs and cutting-edge science help today's Olympic athletes determine how to better their performance through different training strategies, diets and even evaluate how different uniforms can impact performance. Top performing teams have systems in place to track how they are connecting with customers and how products and services are meeting their needs. Creating a system for collecting and analyzing data will help your team see what is working and where you might need to make changes to achieve better performance.

They Celebrate Their Success

Celebrate the wins with your team – big and small! Maybe it's a morning coffee break with treats, a hand written "thank you" card to each member, or a "kudos" article in your company newsletter. It's important your team feel a part of the win.

We all want to be a part of something bigger than ourselves and to feel a part of a winning team – whether in sports, business or in life! We hope you'll be encouraged to use these strategies to build your own gold-medal teams!

■　　■　　■

Meetings that Matter

You've been in them. (You might have even been leading them.) There were great intentions, but at the end of your time together, the general feeling was, "Why did we even bother?"

They are **Meaningless Meetings**. Beyond just an inconvenience they can be a serious waste of organizational resources. (Count up the dollars represented by each attendee losing an hour or more of productivity.)

Contrast that with **Meetings that Matter**. Meetings where crucial decisions and plans are made to move an organization forward. **Meetings that Matter** bring action and results. Here's a quick checklist to consider when planning to attend or organize your next meeting.

Create a Clear Purpose for the Meeting

Write it down for clarity and accountability. What is the objective you want to reach at the end of the meeting? Is it a decision? Is it brainstorming?

Create an Agenda

It's easy to get off track. A clear and concise agenda will help ensure you get through the items you need to discuss and decisions needing to be made.

Start and End on Time

This shows respect for the time of others and helps keep focus if there is a limit to the time allowed for the agenda. End early if you have covered everything on the agenda.

Invite Participants Thoughtfully

Invite only those who really need to attend. For others who may need an update, provide a summary of discussion and action plan after the meeting. (This is a great way to save valuable resources by limiting attendance to just those who *need* to be in meetings.)

Build an Atmosphere that Encourages Creativity and Participation

Encourage participants to come prepared and engage them in the process by asking questions, requesting input and fostering a collaborative environment — one where participants feel their involvement is valued.

Finish With an Action Plan

Determine what action items need to be completed, who will do them and set time-frames. Task someone with following up on the action plan to maximize the value of the meeting.

Evaluate Regular Meetings and Their Effectiveness

Consider if the same decisions or functions could be accomplished in shorter meetings (perhaps a half hour instead of an hour or even the increasing popular brief "stand-up meetings"). Could some of the information discussed or decisions be communicated by email? Consider the cost of the meeting (in terms of lost productivity in other areas while people are attending) and weigh the benefits of moving to a different schedule or format.

Meaningful Meetings can bring valuable ideas and vision to organizations and can clarify next steps to bring great success. By implementing practices to make sure your meetings matter, you'll improve the results of this valuable time investment.

■ ■ ■

Is Your Message Clear?
Effective Communication

Great communication can be the fuel that drives organizations to success. Poor communication skills can quickly derail progress, stall momentum and create obstacles that require valuable resources (time, energy, and money) to overcome.

How is the communication in your organization?
Larger, systemic communication challenges can feel like they are hard to address but solutions can often start one person or one team at a time. If **you** take actions to model positive communication strategies that bring results, others may be more willing to adopt them as well. Here are a few strategies to maximize your communication.

Consider Your Audience

In 1992 President Bush flashed a "peace" sign to Australian farmers in greeting. Instead of a friendly gesture, Australians consider that particular sign as an insult. It's vital we consider our audience when we formulate our messages. Consider the needs, communication style, preferred language (formal vs. informal) and any cultural issues when you are working on a formal letter/request, email, presentation, etc. A bit of thought and research can help ensure your message is received and understood.

Consider Your Communication Mode and Timing

Email can be an incredibly effective tool but don't forget the value of other modes of communication. Phone calls and face-to-face meetings offer additional benefits in connecting with colleagues and stakeholders. Consider the communication preferences of clients and colleagues when it comes to requests, updates and important issues. Having an awareness of individual preferences will help make sure your messages are received and your team is on its way to a successful outcome. (Hint: if you use phone calls or meetings to communicate, be sure to record any items for follow up and transfer them to your action system.)

What Do You Really Want to Say?

When emailing, consider the purpose of your message — does something need to happen? Is there a decision to be made? Are you requesting inform-ation? Is this an update to keep your team in the loop, or do they need to respond? A great tool for clarifying these goals is to use action requests at the beginning of the subject lines of your emails such as, "Confirmation," "Question," or "Action Requested." These will help your audience quickly see any response or actions required on their part to keep communication moving effectively. Be specific in your requests and include due dates for accountability and clarity.

Be a Good Listener

Listening is a key component in effective communication. When talking with others, keep focused and give others your full attention. Avoid interrupting and wait to comment until they have completed sharing their thoughts. Being a good listener encourages and motivates people to also work on their own listening skills.

What is one area you feel could use attention in your communication practices? Take some time to reflect on your strengths and identify areas that could use improvement.

■　　　■　　　■

Building Productive Teams

Productive teams are the heartbeat of growing and thriving organizations. To keep your teams in tip-top shape, practice these fundamentals.

Establish Regular Communication

Checking in is important to make sure projects are on track and that potential obstacles are dealt with in a timely manner.

Delegate and Set Benchmarks for Progress

The best teams work in their strengths and share the load. Consider the strengths of each member as responsibilities are delegated and set a schedule for progress reports along the way.

Minimize Interruptions

While communication is important, avoid long email

chains and excessive use of cc: resulting in overflowing team members' inboxes. Protect your project time by scheduling work sessions on your calendar and letting colleagues know you are unavailable during those times.

Make Your Meetings Matter

Keep meetings on track with a clear agenda and discussion focused on the relevant topics at hand. Create clear action points for follow up. Show respect for your colleagues' time by starting on time and finishing early whenever possible.

Build your best team by modeling productive habits and encouraging others to adopt them as well and watch your organization thrive!

■   ■   ■

PRODUCTIVITY PITFALLS

It is easier to prevent bad habits than to break them.
– Benjamin Franklin

Have you ever walked out to your car to discover a flat tire? It's that sinking feeling knowing you were planning on "going" and circumstances now have you "staying" in one place (at least until you can put on the spare!).

There are those moments when you know you need to get things done and something derails you. These situations are inevitable in any work environment. The key is learning to recover quickly and regain momentum so you can take back your time.

The following are time-proven strategies for avoiding productivity pitfalls and how to get back on track. You too can develop habits and systems that will help you get the most out of each day no matter what "flat tires" come your way!

▨   ▨   ▨

Are You Sabotaging Your Own Productivity?

While we work on some of the external factors to improve our productivity (controlling interruptions, making our **5 Decisions** on incoming information, practicing **Focus Time**, etc.) we can often forget that there are internal issues that impact our productivity as well. If we're not careful, some of these self-imposed "time bombs" can sabotage our efforts.

The Pressure to Multitask

Science tells us that multitasking is truly "switch tasking" — moving from one task to another. Each switch means extra time and effort needed to refocus and complete each of the separate tasks and actually increases potential errors. To really experience higher levels of productivity and efficiency, we must let go of the myth that multitasking is a positive attribute.

Letting Fear Hold You Hostage to Your Inbox

Allowing your work day to be controlled by the flow of email in your inbox is a sure way to hinder your productivity. When we don't turn off our email notifier (afraid that we might miss something), each ding or desktop alert of a new email pulls our attention away from the task at hand. Research says it can take up to 23 minutes after an interruption to get back to the task we were previously working on.[x] Turn off the notifiers and set regular times in the day to check email rather than responding to it all day long. To take even more control of your inbox, minimize it when working on other tasks!

Poor Self-Care

An article in **Inc.** magazine likened an entrepreneur's nutritional needs to that of an athlete in training.[xi] Want to improve your productivity? Fuel yourself with lean proteins, fruits, vegetables and complex carbohydrates while avoiding processed foods and foods high in sugar. Ever feel like you are in the midst of a "brain fog"? It could mean you need to hydrate. The brain is 70-80 percent water and needs optimal hydration to work at its best. Avoid dehydrators like processed sugary foods, high doses of caffeine, and soda. Exercise is also an important investment in making sure you have the energy needed to complete projects.

Difficulty Saying "No"

Productivity can be sabotaged by our best intentions to help others. If we say "yes" to too many good things, none of them get done well. Carefully review your obligations and say "no" to the things you can take off your calendar to make sure you have time to devote to priorities. (This applies at work and at home!) When we say "yes" to something, we are in fact saying "no" to something else. Make sure you are saying "yes" to the right things.

Letting Our Stuff Take Over

Clutter can be a productivity killer. Make efforts to keep work areas clear of distractions and keep the necessary items you need for work in your "target zone" — close enough that you don't have to stop work on projects to go hunting for the tools you need. Invest time in your filing systems (paper and digital) and making sure you are not drowning in piles that slow down your efforts. Practice the "add one, subtract one" tactic. If you add something to your space (work or home) try to get rid of something you no longer need or enjoy to keep your stuff manageable.

Too Much Online Time

Studies say that the average person checks their smart phone 150 times per day![xii] Even if you are only spending an average of one minute each time you are checking your phone, that can add up to over two hours a day! Cut that time in half and you've added one hour back in your day (up to 7 hours per week!) to pursue your passions. Social media pro-grams and mindless internet use can creep into our free time and diminish what's available to pursue things we might love more than checking our friends' Facebook status. Keep tabs on your online time to make sure you are not sabotaging your own productivity with your own technology.

If you struggle with any of these issues, ask a friend or colleague for some accountability to make improvements. Pick one area at a time and set short-term, measurable goals so you can see results that will encourage you to avoid behaviors that may be sabotaging your productivity and keeping you from working at your best.

■　　■　　■

Minimize Distractions

We are never too old to want to "go out and play!" Allow yourself time to play — it's healthy! But to feel good about meeting your goals, create a solid plan of action every day. Focus on getting the most important things done right away so that you can have the option of getting out of the office on time and making the most of your evenings and weekends. Here are some helpful tips for keeping yourself focused.

Remember the Basics to Minimize Distractions

Practice **Focus Time** each day and protect that time by closing your door or putting up your "Do Not Disturb" sign if you work in a cubical. Let your office phone go to voicemail, silence your cell phone, set IM (Instant Messenger) to busy and turn off notifications to keep your focus.

Keep Your Focus on Your Highest Priorities

Don't let lower value, oftentimes easier tasks get in the way of reaching your goals. Use your top three must-do's list to keep you on track.

Make a Game of It

Get past the mental hurdle of trying to keep focused by setting up challenges for yourself. Set a timer and a specific goal for how far you can get on a particular project in 20 minutes. When the timer goes off, take a quick break to stand, stretch, drink some water and then challenge yourself to another 20 minutes. Making it a race against time can take some of the dread and sluggishness out of projects we may not be excited to work on.

Do your best to keep distractions at work at a minimum and you can feel good about the work you've completed. Try these strategies for limiting distractions so you can get out and have fun after work is done!

■   ■   ■

What is Procrastination Costing You?

Procrastination isn't just a harmless character flaw. It can bring serious consequences if left unchecked. Those workouts we put off could bring serious consequences to our health. Putting off that difficult conversation we need to have with a client might be costing our company real dollars. Chronic procrastination can seriously impact our career and might even one day cost us our job. Although the tasks may differ in levels of importance, one thing is sure — there are consequences to procrastination.

So why do we do it so often? Here are just a few reasons we might choose to fill our time with lower value tasks when we want to avoid the more challenging ones.

- **We are a thrill junkie.** Some of us love the rush of the last minute. There's often a rush that comes with feeling like we "scored at the buzzer" with certain tasks or projects.

- **We are a professional avoider with advanced degrees in the area.** We are the ones who are great at justifying the delay of projects by staying busy with other smaller value tasks. A propensity for perfectionism can even make this worse. Our favorite mantra is, "Just let me finish X and then I'll get to Y."

- **We are decision-phobic.** A fear of making the wrong decision or making a mistake keeps us stuck in place. We don't take the time to break a complicated project into small, manageable steps so we just avoid it all together.

There is hope! Working on improving productivity is like exercising a muscle — you can improve strength and endurance to minimize the impact of procrastination in your professional and personal life. Here are a few strategies for getting things done sooner rather than later.

- **Take that first step.** Break the task into bite sized pieces. What is the first step to making a tough phone call? Schedule it on your calendar and start writing a script for the conversation if necessary. Do you have a large report to write? Start with the outline. As the famous saying goes, "Eat that elephant one bite at a time!"

- **Make an appointment with yourself.** Block time on your calendar to work on the project you've been putting off. If it's a large project, block the first hour and before you finish work for that first hour, block the next time you'll come back to the project to make sure you are making progress. Make notes for yourself where you left off so it's easy to know where to begin at your next session.

- **Consider the consequences of delay.** Procrastination increases stress, can be a negative hit on your professional reputation and can drain us of precious time and energy in our busy lives. We can sometimes get un-stuck when we acknowledge energy is going to be spent — do we want to spend it getting the thing done, or avoiding it?

- **Practice flexibility.** The path to finishing a project isn't always a straight one. Anticipate roadblocks and don't let discouragement derail your progress.

- **Find your project's best feature.** It's never hard to find the energy and motivation to do things that we love to do. Find an aspect of the project that is most appealing and start there. Often times, it's the act of getting started that is the most difficult piece.

- **Partner up**. Is there any part of this project that can be shared? Sometimes the isolation of projects is what may be keeping us from getting going. Is there room to invite someone else to participate? The accountability and the collaboration may make it easier to keep the momentum going.

- **Aim for progress, not perfection.** Sometimes a fear of failure is behind our procrastination. If we have unrealistic expectations, this can keep us from getting unstuck on projects that challenge us. When you feel overwhelmed, ask yourself what do you need in order to move forward on the project? More knowledge? Different tools? More time for research? Choose one area and make a goal to make progress in this area and then reevaluate what should come next.

- **Find a reward/motivation system that works for you.** After you set your mini-goals, write down a reward you will allow yourself when you meet them. Maybe it's a movie with a friend or a special lunch out with a coworker or time spent on something you love to do. Be sure to reward yourself for reaching your goals so the motivation is there to keep going on the project.

- **Promise results to others.** Accountability is a powerful weapon in the fight against procrastination. Knowing someone will be asking you if you completed the task might just be the motivation you need to keep on track.

If procrastination is holding you back, consider taking time to identify one of your "big elephants" and try some of these strategies. Soon you'll be enjoying the great reward that comes from crossing it off your to-do list! Make this a season of your life where you start, ***and finish***, a project you have been avoiding, kicking the habit of procrastination to the curb!

■　　■　　■

Tools for Fighting Procrastination

Looking for some tools to help get more done? Here's a list of some popular task management programs. You might consider checking out one of them to help you make progress. *(Disclaimer: these were available at the time of printing. Our apologies if some are offline in the future. We have not tested all of these programs but have reviewed the features of each.)*

Evernote| www.evernote.com

Evernote apps and products make modern life manageable, by letting you easily collect and find everything that matters.

Trello | www.trello.com

Trello is the fastest, easiest way to organize anything, from your day-to-day work, to a favorite side project, to your greatest life plans.

Goodtodo | www.goodtodo.com

A free to-do list that empties your email inbox and improves your productivity.

Listy | www.listy.us

Keep lists online and share them with friends, colleagues and coworkers. Use text, links, pictures and checkboxes to keep track & stay organized.

Nozbe | www.nozbe.com

Nozbe is a tool that helps busy professionals and teams organize time and projects.

Todoist | www.todoist.com

Todoist lets you manage your tasks anywhere. At home. At school. At work. Online. Offline. And on 13 platforms and devices.

Fractal Planner | www.fractalplanner.com

Personal task management software. Take A Complex Project, Job, or Life, and Make It Simple -- FAST!

Teuxdeux | www.teuxdeux.com

A simple "designy" to-do app.

Remember the Milk | www.rememberthemilk.com

Popular reminder/task app. Works with Gmail, Outlook, Evernote and Twitter.

Wunderlist | www.wunderlist.com

Wunderlist provides all the tools to make your goals a reality. Use the simple interface to track everything from grocery shopping to long-term travel plans.

hiTask | www.hitask.com

hiTask is an online task manager and team task list.

Producteev | www.producteev.com

A social task management solution for teams. It's helped thousands of teams get work done faster and more effectively.

■   ■   ■

How to Be Productive in Times of Chaos

Times of crisis and chaos can hit any business or organization. Whether it's a short-term hour or two of craziness or it's an issue that stretches into weeks of diverted efforts, the urgency of chaos and crisis can distract us back into some unproductive work habits if we're not careful. Here are a few tips for staying productive in times of chaos.

Trust Your System

In times of high stress it can be easy to abandon your systems and put out the largest fires first in an effort to speed up your work flow. It may seem like a good idea but moving away from your systems for processing paper, email, action items will mean more work in the long run. Getting behind on projects and daily tasks will only bring more stress. Try to stick to your best practices for productivity even if it feels counter-intuitive to do so in times of crisis and chaos.

Keep to Your Routines

This may seem like an impossible task but as much as you can, try to keep to your established routines (or get back to them as soon as you can) to ensure your optimal productivity. Keep up with healthy habits related to sleep, fitness and nutrition as much as you can. Getting sick will do nothing to help you get through the busy times at work and in life.

"Bookmark" Your Projects

If a crisis or urgent matter needs your attention, be sure to note where you are in your regular projects so you can pick back up where you left off when things settle down. Be sure to keep coworkers and clients updated on delays that might occur due to the urgent matters you are needing to address. Good communication can help ensure there are fewer frustrations if deadlines need to be adjusted.

Take a Lesson From the Scouts: Be Prepared

When the days are delightfully "normal," take some time to make contingency plans that will help in times of crisis. Prepare instructions for tasks you might be able to delegate to others when your attention needs to be elsewhere. Get ahead on projects and tasks in anticipation of dealing with urgent matters. Make sure you are keeping up on supplies you'll need for projects (paper, printer ink, binders, presentation folders, etc.).

Try a few of these strategies and hopefully next time you are faced with crisis or chaos, you'll be able to sail through the storm and come out without losing any productivity on the other side.

■　　■　　■

Plugging those Pesky Time Leaks

Like an open window in winter can suck the warmth out of your home, **time leaks** in our routines can sabotage productivity efforts at work. Here are a few common ones and some strategies to replace them with positive alternatives.

Time Leak #1 – The Internet

The internet is a wonderful glorious thing, kind of like mint chocolate chip ice cream. But we all know, too much of a good thing and suddenly, it can become very bad for us. Time online that is not work-centered can be a major time leak in our day that keeps us from important projects. If you struggle in this area, try setting some boundaries by limiting yourself to checking social media, news sites and other favorites at set times each day or use a timer to keep track of time. Struggling with your will power to truly unplug? There are programs available that will allow you to disconnect from the internet for set periods of time (Freedom www.macfreedom.com)[xiii]. While you're offline, use **Capture Cards** to note tasks you need to do online when your "unplugged" time is finished.

Time Leak #2 - Multitasking

Once celebrated as a necessary skill, modern science has demonstrated that our accuracy and efficiency truly suffer when we try to multitask. The same two projects that would have taken 30 minutes had we done them one at a time, might end up taking up to twice as long when we are trying to do them at the same time. Add up those minutes over the span of a month and you can lose a significant amount of time if you don't address this leak. Take steps to intentionally work on one project at a time.

Time Leak #3 - Interruptions

Many of us work in busy environments and a significant challenge can be the interruptions from coworkers, clients and vendors who need attention (either in person, on the phone or through email).

Use strategies like turning off your email notifiers, shutting your door, forwarding calls to voicemail (if that's an option) and blocking your schedule for some **Focus Time**, to plug the time leaks that come from a busy environment.

Time Leak #4 - Poor Planning

Not having a plan for the day means you'll likely spend more time reacting and less time making intentional choices about where you are investing your time. This can be a major source of time leaking out of your schedule. Suddenly, it's the end of the day and you wonder where it went! Invest a few minutes at the end of each day creating a plan for the next day. What are the three "must do" activities or projects that are the highest priority for your attention? Place the list (digital or paper) where you will see it first thing the next day.

Time Leak #5 - Extended Socializing at Work

People are important and building relationships with your coworkers is vital to having a positive work environment. However, the time we spend catching up on our favorite reality TV shows while refilling our coffee at the office kitchen can really add up. Watch out for time leaks in some of your extended, non-work related conversations. Instead, consider taking a walk with a coworker at lunch or meeting at the gym after work to catch up on families and favorite past times so you can focus on work projects during work hours.

Keeping these time leaks under control can help ensure you're not wasting energy always trying to play catch up with important projects. Watch for these slow leaks and make sure they don't suck the energy out of your days!

■　　■　　■

Bust the Clutter!

It creeps into all areas of our life and can be a real productivity downer. It's clutter — the stuff that seems to collect on bare surfaces, wind up in piles and can take our time away from higher priority projects. We had good intentions for this "stuff," but now it seems to be taking more and more time to keep organized and in control. Before we throw our hands up in surrender, check out some tips for busting the clutter in some of the areas of our lives.

Clutter Busters for the Office

- Keep frequently used items close and store other tools and resources away from your work area.
- Use containers and drawer dividers to keep smaller items in place (Post-its®, paper clips, thumb drives, extra cords).

- Purge documents, journals and things you don't need so they don't take over your workspace. Create digital scans of items you think you might need later and then purge the paper.

- It's great to have personal items near your workstation to inspire you but limit photos and mementos so they don't take over your workspace. Cycle different ones in every few months for a change of scenery.

- Schedule time each week for filing so piles don't take over the flat surfaces of your desk and work area.

Clutter Busters for Your Car

- Store emergency items in a small plastic bin in the trunk. Don't forget an old blanket, ice scraper, jumper cables, flares and a flashlight. (Other helpful items are hand sanitizer, a few bottles of water and granola bars.)

- Keep important documents, a pen and scratch pad in a coupon organizer in your glove box.

- Develop a system for garbage and empty it each time you fill up for gas. (Removable 3M

Command Hooks with a plastic bag are a great option to keep the garbage from rolling around on the floor.)

- Set up technology for **safe**, **hands-free** use in the car **before** you use it. A voice recording app or digital recorder can also be helpful to dictate notes and reminders when you are traveling.

Clutter Busters at Home

- Put a "donate" box by the door and make a goal to fill it each week with items you no longer use or need.

- Process mail before you lay it on a flat surface.

- Purge any magazines older than three months. (If you haven't read it yet, chances are you likely won't. Pass them on to gyms, senior centers or schools for reuse.)

- Create a "launch" zone for easier mornings. Give each member of the family a basket or bin to put items they need for the day (work-out clothes, laptops, back-packs, library books, lunches, etc.).

- Use hooks, shelves and containers to hang, stash, and hide items.
- File instruction books and warranties in an A-Z accordion folder or binder by appliance name (T for toaster, C for coffee maker, etc.).
- Store out-of-season shoes and clothes and purge when you switch seasons. Donate items that don't fit or you no longer wear.

Keep clutter from sabotaging your productivity by creating habits and environments that keep things SIMPLIFIED!

▪　▪　▪

TAKING CARE OF YOU!

The simplification of life is one of the steps to inner peace. A persistent simplification will create an inner and outer well-being that places harmony in one's life.
–Peace Pilgrim

Stress is a vicious cycle. A 2013 survey by the American Psychological Association's Center for Organizational Excellence found that **more than one-third of working Americans experience chronic work-related stress.**[xiv]

We feel stressed because we have so much to do. That stress negatively impacts our productivity and focus slowing us down and making us prone to errors and mistakes. We get further behind, more stressed and the cycle continues. It can even impact our health. Stress has been called the health epidemic of the 21st century and more evidence is coming to light that it is a factor in several of the most serious diseases we are facing in today's culture. Stress costs us peace of mind, our health and has a hefty price tag when you start calculating health care costs, absences and lost productivity.

Taking care of ourselves isn't just a **nice** idea – it's **necessary** in today's 24/7 culture. In order to stay healthy, have fulfilled lives and to maintain the energy and focus to meet our personal and professional goals, we need to invest in self-care.

Learn to make decisions and choices to take care of YOU even in the busiest times at work (and at home). The goal is to protect your most valuable resource – time – and help you live a life SIMPLIFIED!

■   ■   ■

Staying Productive
During the Holidays

Plates of baked goods in the break room, ugly Christmas sweater parties, Secret Santa gift exchanges — celebrating the holidays at work has traditions that are as sacred as Aunt Mary's mystery Jell-O salad.

However, in today's competitive workplace, it's more important than ever to keep focus and momentum on the job. No one wants to be a Grinch and hide out in her cubicle for the month of December, but how do you keep focus when the office is swept up in holiday buzz? Here are some tips to help you stay off the boss's naughty list during the holiday season.

Give Your Calendar Extra Attention

- Take extra time to track meetings and appointments on a paper or digital calendar.

- Add any holiday events such as luncheons, parties, etc. and take care of RSVPs as soon as possible.

- Track the holiday schedules of others that might impact your workflow. Anticipate decisions and input you might need from colleagues before they leave for holiday vacations. Do your part to make sure you are not bothering them on their time away and they'll likely return the favor.

- Check in with vendors for their holiday schedules. Adjust deadlines to cover for holiday closures/shipping issues.

- If you are planning time away from the office make sure coworkers have what they need to cover your duties and follow through on projects while you are gone.

A Gift From You, To You - Schedule Focus Time

- The Pareto Principle says we get 80% of the work of our day done in 20% of our day. If you work an 8-hour day, that's 96 minutes. Consider "booking" that time in your own schedule every day, to work on projects without interruptions. This time more than just a gift – it's necessary in allowing you to get the right things done instead of being distracted and making little or no progress on your higher value work.

- To protect your **Focus Time**, turn off email notifications, stay offline, put your phone on "do not disturb" and hang a sign on your door that lets coworkers know when you'll be available. Consider this time a gift – allowing you to get the right things done instead of being distracted and making little or no progress on your higher value work.

- Watch out for multitasking. Once touted as the secret weapon of busy professionals, research shows this practice actually reduces our efficiency and can produce substandard work. Thinking you can shop for little Jimmy's Christmas gift during the sales meeting might seem like a great use of your time, but may come back to bite you later on when you're asked to provide a summary of the meeting.

A Fresh Start is Around the Corner

- What are some areas you want to work on for the future? Write down goals for the first quarter of the New Year (keeping them shorter term will help you measure and track your progress).
- If your schedule allows, consider taking time around the holidays to purge and physically organize your work space. (This includes digital files — can documents be moved to archives?)
- Setting up new folders (digital and paper) for the New Year can make it easier to hit the ground running after the holidays.

Approach December with some intention and planning and you just might finish the month with the greatest gift of all — a clean desk and completed projects!

■   ■   ■

Simple Gift Giving Ideas

Looking for ideas to keep gift giving simple? For some, giving gifts during the holidays, birthdays and special occasions can be an unnerving process. You don't want to add to the clutter and "stuff" your family, friends and colleagues must manage but you want to express love and appreciation and celebrate the occasion. Before you buy your dad his 99th necktie or give your mom another scarf, consider some of these gifts that won't be stuck in a drawer or on a shelf gathering dust.

Give Consumable Gifts

Choose one of their favorite snacks, home-made treats, a favorite bottle of wine or a basket of fresh fruit. This helps everyone cut down on excess clutter and items that aren't really needed.

Give Experiences That You Can Share

Gift certificates for classes, performances, sporting events and other kinds of experiences can make a great gift. The events don't need to take place right away — look ahead to events that might happen in the months beyond the giving of the gift. Sometimes the anticipation is part of the fun!

Give a Gift That Encourages Their Passions

Do they love photography? Consider a photography lesson or a gift certificate to have their favorite images published in a photo book. Do they love to cook? See if you can find a local cooking class. Some ideas might be books related to their interests, tools, materials, equipment or classes that will help them move forward in their hobbies. Look to the internet or reputable retailers if you need assistance.

The Gift of Time Can Be the Most Valuable One of All!

Instead of opting for a restaurant gift card for your team or staff, take them to lunch. Sharing a meal and making sure the conversation is not all work-based allows you to build relationships and express appreciation for their contributions. For family members, plan a special time together doing something you'll all enjoy. It's not so much the activity as the investment in the relationships that is the greatest gift!

Give to Serve Others

Instead of exchanging gifts with friends and colleagues during the holidays, research opportunities to partner with them to serve others. Food banks, homeless shelters and other charitable organizations can always use extra resources and help during the holiday season (or really any season).

Give to Inspire

Do you have a favorite book that has provided an "ah ha" moment? Consider giving a copy and a note about how it changed your life/perspective/attitude. The gifts of wisdom and inspiration are some of the best we can give to those we love and appreciate!

Make gift giving an act of great joy and fun instead feeling it's a stressful effort to find just the right thing. A bit of time engaged in thoughtful gifts that don't contribute to clutter and express your appreciation will help SIMPLIFY! your gift giving at any time of the year!

※　　※　　※

Ready for a break? Staying Productive During Vacation Season

Whether you have plans for an exotic vacation or a thrifty "stay-cation", one of the biggest challenges of a vacation is catching up after you return. Here are a few tips to make sure your post-vacation Zen isn't cut short from productivity challenges at work.

Cushion Your Calendar

Note any deadlines that need to be met before you leave and schedule time to complete these projects or request extensions if necessary before you leave. Double check that payments, deliveries and other time sensitive duties are either automated or delegated in your absence. If possible, reschedule meetings that occur right before and right after your time out of the office. (Keep in mind that the world probably won't stop turning if something needs to be rescheduled. Work is important but spending time with loved ones and refueling your "tank" is important, too!)

Delegate Duties

Carefully check deadlines and projects and make sure you've arranged for adequate coverage while you are away. Try to anticipate what clients, vendors and others might need and leave a list of contacts who can field calls and manage requests while you are gone. Ensuring that things are covered in your absence will make for an easier first week back in the office when you return!

Set Your Email Auto Reply and Voicemail Message

Make sure that they include information about who to contact for urgent requests/issues in your absence and when you'll be returning messages.

Set Clear Boundaries

There are times we may need to check email or follow up on work items when on vacation. If you must check in with the office, set clear boundaries with your coworkers on when you will be available (for example, one hour in the morning or one hour in the evening). Set the same time frame for yourself for checking in with the office so you don't squander away your precious vacation time!

Take a Technology Vacation

Many of us work in technology saturated jobs where we are "on" several hours each day. Give your brain a break and try to unplug as much as possible while on vacation. Plan activities that don't require screen time and challenge yourself to give your personal devices a vacation as well (even though it can be tempting to check emails and voicemails if we always have access).

Block Focus Time for Your Return

It's not reasonable to expect you could be gone for several days and expect to catch up on all your work the first day you are back. Be proactive and plan ahead! Before you depart, make sure you schedule several blocks of time after you return to batch process emails, voicemails and requests that came in while you were gone.

Consider Scheduling a "Soft" Return

Add a day or two to your auto responder (voice and email) so you can catch up with work for a day or two before feeling like people might expecting to call or connect with you.

Plan for fun days and experiences that will build great memories when you take time away from work. It's always good to take breaks and the anticipation of time away can often keep us motivated and energized on some of the more challenging days!

◼   ◼   ◼

Scheduling for Success at Home

Keeping life simple at home helps reduce stress in all areas of your life. If you are looking to tackle some organizing projects at home, here are a few ideas you can usually finish in a weekend. Block the time to work on them and put it on your calendar for accountability.

- Pare down your kitchen supplies. (Do you really need three colanders?) Take extras or items you don't need to a local charity.

- As you swap out your summer clothes for fall and winter, challenge yourself to get rid of the items you didn't wear at all this summer. Donate the items to charity so someone else can enjoy them.

- Donate coats, sweaters and blankets you and your family no longer use to area shelters so people can have them in time for cold weather.

- Purge the magazines and books you no longer need. Look for organizations who might take them as donations.
- Start collecting tax receipts and document-tation so you'll be ready to tackle taxes early this year.
- Choose an area of the garage to clean and organize. Check the status of your tools and supplies for household chores. Toss those that are in disrepair or no longer needed. Look for items that need special handling for recycling (cleaners, paint, electronics, metals, chemicals, etc.). Gather them and take them to organizations that can dispose of them safely.

Motivate yourself to take on these projects by promising yourself a reward when they are done. Schedule a movie night, a date at your favorite restaurant or a special treat when you check these projects off your weekend to-do list. Controlling the clutter and disorganization at home is an important way to make sure you are taking care of YOU!

■   ■   ■

Making Time to Live Your Passions

If you've been working on improving your processes and systems at work (and at home) to get the right things done with less stress, pursuing your passions is an important element in that equation. Research and experience teach us that "down time" is vital to developing critical thinking and problem solving skills for our professional lives.

Taking time to pursue our passions and things we love to do is not just a "nice" thing anymore. It's *necessary* for overall health and well-being. The benefits to our lives stretch beyond just health. Pursuing our passions (at work or in our free time) can have direct impact on our productivity and happiness. Wondering how to jump off the "hamster wheel" of life to pursue your passions? Here are a few tips for making time for the things you love to do.

Dream-Storm

Do you ever fantasize about what you'd do if time and money were unlimited? Take a few minutes to write these dreams down. What would you do? Travel? Make a special purchase? Volunteer at your favorite charity?

Write three activities down on a Post-it® note and place it somewhere you can see them. Those are either your passions or steps to discovering your true passions. Identifying them and keeping them visible reminds you to make them a priority in your life. Look at your list for cues to discover your true passions. Maybe you won't be able to buy that classic roadster to park in your own driveway but you could attend a local car show or browse through a collector's magazine. Perhaps the 7-day Caribbean cruise isn't a possibility but a day-cruise on your city's local waterway will give you a great relaxing day on the water. Look for ways to pursue your passion in baby steps.

Take Back Your Time

Many people don't pursue their passion because they say they don't have the time. According to a Nielsen ratings study, **the average American watches about 35 hours of television every week!**[xv] Another time black hole for many folks - Facebook. **The average user spends about 40 minutes a day on Facebook. That adds up to about 20 hours per month on Facebook**. With 968 million daily active users on average, we know that means a lot of you![xvi]

If keeping up with your favorite shows or looking at your friend's vacation photos are your passions, great! Enjoy that outlet. *But if you find yourself sitting in front of the TV or computer out of laziness and boredom, consider taking back that time and investing it in your passion.* Take a class, join a club or volunteer for an organization where you can pursue what you love.

Schedule a Date With Your Passion.

Reserving time in your schedule to do what you love to do will keep it from being pushed out of the way by other obligations. If your passion is fitness, sign up for a race or class that will help you learn new skills or train for an event. If reading is a passion, find a book club that meets in your area. Are you passionate about cooking? Sign up for a class to sharpen your skills. Do you love being outdoors? Block time this summer for day trips to some new locations that will get you outside. Better yet, make plans with a friend who shares your passions and you'll be even more likely to keep the date!

Invest In Your Passion

Making a time or financial commitment is a great way to hold yourself accountable to pursuing your passions. Even small purchases can be a great inspiration.

If you're a gardener, maybe it's a new pair of gardening gloves. If fitness is your passion, perhaps it's signing up for a race or event where you will have to commit to putting in the time to train. The financial commitment doesn't need to be huge, but when you've put some money in, you will likely be more inclined to put some time in to pursing that passion as well.

Your interests and passions play an important role in creating the energy for your every-day tasks and responsibilities. Make conscious decisions to invest in yourself and spend time doing things you love!

Try Some New Passions.

It's never too late to try new hobbies and experiences. The experiences can help you translate some of that adventurous spirit into speaking up with new ideas and learning new skills for your professional life as well.

A Little Can Go a Long Way

Busy week? Don't worry about finding an hour or two at a time. Look for 15 minutes to take a walk, listen to music or read a few pages from a favorite author. Remember these small doses of filling your passion-tank can be just as effective.

Taking time to pursue your passions is an important part of investing in your health and wellness. The time spent on hobbies, projects and things you love to do can help you manage stress levels and fill your "tank" with valuable energy resources for busy days at work.

■　　　■　　　■

Energize Naturally

Wouldn't it be great if we could recharge as easily as some of our devices? Plugging in to get our personal batteries from "empty" to "full" by simply flipping a switch would make life so much easier! In reality, maintaining energy to meet professional and personal obligations is an ongoing challenge for almost everyone. Here are some strategies for keeping energy levels high at work and at home.

Fuel Your Body with Healthy Foods and Water

Avoid unnatural energy boosters such as high sugar snacks, caffeine and chemical energy supplements. These can add wear and tear on your body and contribute to chronic health conditions when you use them in excess. Keep healthy snacks available to avoid temptations to hit the vending machines or the left-over birthday cake in the break room.

Move More

We are learning more about the serious health consequences tied to sitting for extended periods of time. Get up and move throughout your day as much as possible. Try to take a 10-20-minute walk after lunch to boost your levels of dopamine, norepi-nephrine, and serotonin, all of which will give you more energy when you return to work. Practice easy stretches you can do quickly at your desk which can help you refocus on work.

Plan Ahead

A day spent in "reactive" mode can quickly drain your batteries. Start your day with a clear plan and do your best to stick to it even when interruptions come your way. Knowing your goals for the day can help you keep focus and keep energy levels consistent rather than allowing them to spike and drop.

Let There Be Light

Work to get some "natural light" time. If your office doesn't have windows be sure to use breaks and lunch times to get outside (even on cloudy and rainy days) to let the natural light help regulate your body energy rhythms.

Unplug and Take Breaks

Breaks and time away from work are an important part of recharging. In order to bring our best efforts the next day, avoid bringing work home in the evenings and be sure to get the rest you need. It's important to turn off electronic devices (laptops, tablets and phones) one hour before bedtime to ensure you get quality rest.

Strategies to energize naturally will boost your efforts in focus and productivity. Make choices that will give you the energy you need to pursue your professional and personal goals!

▓   ▓   ▓

Healthy Habits for Productivity

It's a good idea to regularly take time to evaluate if some of your health choices may be impacting your overall productivity. As you are implementing positive strategies at work to improve productivity (**Focus Time**, **Capture Cards**, blocking time for batching tasks, etc.) it may be helpful to look at health choices you can make to give you even more of an edge.

Smart Fuel

Many of us know that eating healthy, whole foods is good for our health but it can be good for our productivity as well. If this is an area you feel you could improve, consider experimenting with these following changes:

- Don't skip breakfast! Find something that works well to prepare quickly and will give you the energy to start your day strong. Try smoothies, oatmeal or eggs.

- Drink up! Your brain really needs water to work at its best. Brain fuzziness and mental fatigue can be a symptom of early dehydration. Keep a water bottle at your desk and make it a goal to refill it at least a few times during the day.

- Pack your lunch. It gives you control and will help you avoid the temptation to opt for "fast" food which is often highly processed and may leave you feeling sluggish.

- Don't eat at your desk. Get away for a break from your workspace so you can return refreshed.

- Bring healthy snacks to work. Fresh fruit, almonds, high fiber crackers and even string cheese sticks can give a great boost when you need energy.

The Link Between Fitness and Focus

According to the World Health Organization (WHO), 60 to 85% of the population worldwide does not engage in enough activity and are leading a sedentary lifestyle.[xvii] Exercise influences our health, energy, mood and ability to focus. We know this can be a challenge in our busy, overwhelmed lives but ask yourself, *would you rather spend 30 minutes moving and taking care of your body or an extra hour on your work because you are struggling to focus?* If this is a challenge for you, consider these tips:

- Sitting for extended periods of time is now believed to be as harmful to our health as smoking! If possible, consider walking or stand-up meetings as options. Stand while on phone calls. Take the stairs or park further from your office if possible.

- Consider a pedometer app for your phone or one that you can wear and set a personal goal for daily steps. A walk at lunch and a walk for an afternoon break can often help you make great progress toward that goal each day.

- Schedule time for exercise like you would an appointment. Ask a friend to help keep you accountable and set short-term goals that will help you keep momentum.

Good Nights for Productive Days

Our productivity can take a big hit if we are not getting enough sleep. Here are some strategies for getting a good night's rest:

- Turn off ALL electronics at least an hour before bed. Give your brain time to wind down and get ready for sleep.
- Keep electronics out of the bedroom so your rest will be uninterrupted by beeps and buzzes!
- Avoid caffeine late in the day to make sure you can fall asleep easily.
- Keep a stack of **Capture Cards** and a pen on your bedside table so if you remember something you need to do, you can make note of it and not worry through the night.

A healthy lifestyle is vital to be around for the things that are most important to you — your family, friends and energy to pursue your true passions. A bonus is that healthy life choices can play a part in helping you improve productivity at work as well.

Here's to good healthy food, getting outside and sweet dreams of productive days ahead!

The Importance of White Space

In the world of document design, there is a concept called "white space." Designers will work strategically to keep some space without text and graphics. It's an important design tool to make sure messaging is clear and balanced. Without white space, readers might be tempted to just skip over the important messages because of overwhelming clutter.

In our busy daily lives "white space" can be the time that we allow ourselves a bit of rest and renewal. In today's 24/7 world, finding this time can often be a challenge. Here are some tips for keeping white space in our schedules.

Schedule Your Down Time Like You Would a Meeting

Just as it's important to schedule **Focus Time**, there's

value in scheduling down time as well. It's easy for responsibilities and obligations to creep into our free time but if the time is blocked or reserved on our calendars, the creep is easier to control. Spontaneity is important, but scheduling your "me" time will help lock it in.

Make Specific Plans for Your Down Time

Choose activities you know will refresh and renew you (instead of putting further stress and drain on your life). A great motivator to keep that time reserved is to invest in that time in advance: purchase tickets for a play, pay an entrance fee for a race or event, or at the very least, make a commitment to a friend or family member to go for a hike, pack a picnic or pick a local site to visit that will get you out and about and away from things that feel like work or chores.

Evaluate Your Extracurricular Activities

A lack of white space in your life might be coming from an overbooked calendar that doesn't allow you time to refuel for busy work weeks. If you find yourself involved in obligations that zap your energy rather than filling you up, consider reducing or eliminating those activities.

Watch Your Online Time

Today it's easier than ever to zone out with online activities. Watch out for these activities that might masquerade as white space but really don't do much to refuel and refresh you. Set limits (especially on evenings and weekends) for screen time. Consider keeping a timer around and if you are going to indulge in a bit of Netflix, YouTube or Facebook, set a time limit.

If this is an area of struggle, try some of these strategies to add white space to your life. It can do amazing things to help your overall productivity!

■   ■   ■

Adding and Changing Habits

As you learn new strategies for improving your productivity, how do you go about changing old unproductive habits to new ones that allow you to get more done in less time with less stress? Here are strategies that can help when you are working to change a habit or start a new one.

Have a Clear Purpose

To be successful in changing or adding a new habit, it's important to know WHY you want to make the change. Knowing the WHY will make for a greater rate of success. Do you want to spend less time looking for things? Get the promotion you've been dreaming of? Are you tired of being late? When you struggle with implementing the new habit, remember the WHY!

One at a Time

A quick way to fail at setting new habits is to try to take on too many at once. For best results, focus on changing one habit at a time. Start small and start slow so you can build momentum to really make the changes stick.

Write it Down

Articulate exactly what you are hoping to change and give yourself a timeline. If you are working on limiting how much time you are in your email, make appointments with yourself on your calendar for when you'll check your inbox. Using your calendar adds a level of commitment to something you want to change.

Identify Your Triggers and Potential Obstacles

The best offense can be a strong defense when working to change unproductive habits. What causes you to slip into the unproductive behaviors? Is it not having a plan? Looking for distractions? Feeling overwhelmed? Identify some of your triggers and what you can do to replace them with positive behaviors.

Set a 30-day Challenge

New habits take time to build. By setting yourself up to give the habit at least a 30-day try, you give yourself time to build the new behavior into a habit.

Invest in the New Habit

We are more likely to stick with something if we have a bit of "skin in the game." If you have invested in training or equipment that will help you in developing the new habit, it may be a good motivation to keep at it on the more difficult days.

Ask for Help

Accountability can be an excellent strategy for successfully changing habits. Share your goals with a colleague or friend and check in regularly to share your progress and challenges. Accountability to yourself and others will help you find success.

Don't Let Setbacks Stop You

Regroup and learn from your slip-ups. Reevaluate

your triggers and obstacles and make sure you have systems in place to help you succeed. Remember, you can hit reset and start again when you have a difficult day.

Reward Yourself

When you feel the new habit is officially part of your routine, reward yourself and celebrate your hard work. It doesn't have to cost anything — your reward could be that you take some time to do something you love!

Investing in habits that will SIMPLIFY! your life will help you find your best life/work balance. It can be a challenge but the results are worth it!

■   ■   ■

Need to Unplug?

With 24/7 access, it can be tempting to spend hours online when we don't really need to. Recently a news report highlighted a new condition called "text neck" that develops from looking at screens too much! If one of your goals is to unplug more often, here are some tips to keep you on track.

Put Some Distance Between You and Your Technology

Often our urge to connect comes out of the purely habitual practice of having technology at hand. Challenge yourself to put your phone in your desk drawer or in your bag while at work instead of always having it at hand. The distance will help you break habits of using technology as a self-imposed interruption when you are finding it hard to focus. (If this is hard to do, it reinforces that you may have a problem with being too attached to your tech!)

Give Yourself a Curfew

Set a time each evening that will be "lights out" for your technology. Studies show that late night use is one of the key culprits of poor sleep patterns. Charge your phone in a room other than your bedroom to ensure you're not tempted to check it after you've turned in for the night.

Read Without Using Technology Every Day

We can find lots of great info online and e-readers are a wonderful convenience (we love ours!) but reading other types of print resources can give you a valuable break from screen time. Consider a book, magazine or journal that may not be available online that will fuel your passions and interests. The public library can be a great resource for books, magazines and journals that may not be available online that will fuel your passions and interests without costing you a dime.

Make Connections Without Technology

Make a commitment to connect with people live and

in person! Make a lunch date, take a walk, make a phone call or send a card to one work colleague and one family friend each week. It's important to the health of our relationships to invest more than just a few characters on a screen in an email, text or Facebook post.

Partner With Someone for Accountability

If unplugging and improving your tech habits seems harder than you thought, try the buddy system. It's always easier to tackle challenges with someone cheering you on! Find a friend or family member and share your best "unplugged" strategies.

Some days will be easier than others. Don't give up if you have a day where you fall to the temptation to spend extra hours online. Just start fresh the next day. The aim is to take back some of the time technology sucks from our daily lives with mindless activities. Step away from your screens and enjoy your time doing what you love!

Boost Your Brain Power

Productivity isn't just about what we take out of our daily tasks and duties. It's often about how we invest our time that makes the long-term changes in how much we can get done in a day. One of the best ways to invest your time is to increase your knowledge and experience in areas that will match the skills you use every day. Here are a few tips to boost your brain power and your productivity.

Identify 3-5 Critical Areas You Want to Improve

Are there tasks that take more time than you know they should? Perhaps it's administrative tasks like managing email or keeping on top of the paper flow of your work. Maybe it's preparing presentations or public speaking. Is there a software program you use that you know you are not getting the most from in your projects? Make a list of some of the areas you know you could take back some time in your weeks if you just had a bit more training or knowledge.

Take a Class

Trainings can be valuable especially if they offer some hands-on exercises to help you implement what you learn. Options might include a one-day training either on- or off-site, or a longer term commitment to a class (several weeks). Research options within your organization for training resources. If no resources are available or you are in business for yourself, look for local organizations, community colleges or business association offerings that might match what you are looking for. Other options may be webinars or online learning opportunities that last just an hour or two.

Look for Other Resources

There are plenty of other options for improving your skills. Check out videos on YouTube and blogs that may help you acquire the skills you need (especially for topics related to popular software programs and social media). If you belong to a professional association, see if they also have resources available to members that might help you learn or refine professional skills. Check your local library for books, journals and other resources that might help as well.

Find an Expert

You have probably heard the old adage: If you want to get better at something, surround yourself with people who do it better than you. Spend time with people who are skilled in the areas you want to develop. Find out what books they read, what professional organizations they belong to, what classes they've attended. Emulate these as much as possible. Consider asking one of these people to be a mentor. Learn from the best!

Use Your New Skills

To ensure you get the most from the time you invest put your new skills to work right away and schedule specific times to practice what you have learned. Set goals to implement new skills in current and future projects and ask for accountability from colleagues if that helps.

Share Your own Expertise with Others

It can be a powerful resource for an organization when their own staff shares knowledge and skills with colleagues. It fosters team-building and maximizes the resources of the organization. Improving the profound knowledge of the team will help ensure high-value projects receive the time and attention they deserve as well as reducing the risk of burn-out and turnover among teams. If you work in a solo environment, there may be others in your networks you could teach in exchange for their own expertise in certain areas.

Select One Area and Commit to Improving Your Knowledge

Choose one of the critical areas you identified and take time to look at ways you can invest in boosting your brain power for more productive days ahead.

■　　■　　■

About the Authors

Bethanne Kronick is passionate about helping people live with less stress and find more time and energy. Bethanne established SIMPLIFY! in 2002. She offers classes and workshops to businesses and organizations on a variety of topics related to focus, organizing and productivity. Bethanne is also a keynote speaker and presenter. She is a member of the National Speaker's Association (NSA), a Certified Professional Organizer (CPO) and a member of the National Association of Professional Organizers (NAPO). In her spare time, Bethanne is a competitive rower and loves to eat ice cream!

Kim Greenwood is driven to help make sure messages are clear and relevant. She has been honored to work with a variety of for- and non-profit organizations in the area of communications over the years. Her primary role with SIMPLIFY! is to make sure the important messages and strategies make it to people looking to cut clutter and improve productivity in their lives. As a self-described "word geek," she is amazed and thankful that she's found a career that lets her read and write as a part of her job! In her free time she loves to spend time with family, explore new Portland culinary hot-spots and dabbles enough in crafty hobbies to be dangerous around a glue gun.

Share your stories...

We hope you've been encouraged by this book! Productivity isn't necessarily a destination but a journey. We would welcome hearing your stories of success and how making The ***SIMPLIFY! Collection*** a part of your daily life has helped you on your journey. Drop us a note at:

P.O. Box 443, Camp Sherman, OR, 97730

or info@simplifynw.com.

Gratitude

Bethanne – Thank you to my many wonderful clients who motivate me to continue to develop concepts and content to share. It's through your utilizing this information and SIMPLIFY!'ing your lives that drives my desire to develop and offer even more! The successes that I've seen in people's lives becoming streamlined, simplified, happier, less stressed and more joyful are astounding. This book is for you!

An inordinate amount of thanks goes to Kim. Your creativity and writing talents are such a huge part of SIMPLIFY!'s success. Your drive and persistence to complete this project have been off the charts. I am very grateful to you as well as your family for the times that you put SIMPLIFY! first.

Dave, thank you, as always, for your endless support of my journey to help SIMPLIFY! the lives of others. Having you by my side makes it do-able and certainly more fun!

Kim – Thanks to Bethanne for the opportunity to work on this great project. I love thinking about all the people who will take back their time with the strategies in this book! Thanks to Brad, Natalie and J.T. for their unwavering support and encouraging me to pursue my own passions in work and life. And special thanks to my 9th grade English teacher who was the first to tell me I could write well. I hope she'd be pleased to know I found a way to keep on practicing all she taught me.

Endnotes

[i] You can find **SIMPLIFY! One Day at a Time** at
www.simplifynw.com

[ii] These websites are current as of printing. Our suggestions
are not endorsements, just options for review.

[iii] We can't personally vouch for these sites but wanted to
offer them as a resource. Please use caution and do your
research before signing on with a ride-share or carpool
program. Safety first!

[iv] Saving energy by powering down computers:
http://preview.www.thedailygreen.com/going-
green/tips/energy-efficiency-turn-computer-off

[v] Office Depot Green Buying Guide:
http://www.officedepot.com/a/guides/buygreen/buygreen/

[vi] The average professional spends up to 28 percent of their
work week on emails
http://www.mckinsey.com/insights/high_tech_telecoms_inte
rnet/the_social_economy

[vii] People check their smartphones an average of 150 times
per day: http://communities-
dominate.blogs.com/brands/2013/01/an-attempt-to-
validate-the-150x-per-day-number-based-on-typical-
user.html

[viii] Value of time lost in the US due to social media:
http://mashable.com/2012/11/02/social-media-work-
productivity/

[ix] Freedom – disconnect from the internet for set periods of
time. Basic version is free but a
version with extra features can be purchased.
https://freedom.to/

[x] "Worker, Interrupted: The Cost of Task Switching" by Kermit Pattison, http://www.fastcompany.com/944128/worker-interrupted-cost-task-switching

[xi] "You Lead as You Eat," Adam Bluestein, July/August 2013, http://www.inc.com/magazine/201307/adam-bluestein/the-best-foods-for-leaders-to-eathtml.html

[xii] People check their smartphones an average of 150 times per day: http://communities-dominate.blogs.com/brands/2013/01/an-attempt-to-validate-the-150x-per-day-number-based-on-typical-user.html

[xiii] Freedom – disconnect from the internet for set periods of time. Basic version is free but a version with extra features can be purchased. https://freedom.to/

[xiv] American Psychological Association's Center for Organizational Excellence http://www.apa.org/news/press/releases/2013/03/employee-needs.aspx

[xv] Average American watches 35 hours of television per week: http://www.fool.com/investing/general/2015/03/15/the-average-american-watches-this-much-tv-every-da.aspx

[xvi] Statistics on Facebook: http://www.adweek.com/socialtimes/social-media-minutes-day/503160, http://newsroom.fb.com/company-info/

[xvii] According to the World Health Organization (WHO), 60 to 85% of the population worldwide does not engage in enough activity and are leading a sedentary lifestyle: http://www.who.int/mediacentre/factsheets/fs385/en/